TH

J. W. Carey.

THE CAREYS

Honor Rudnitzky

Blackstaff Press

Published by Blackstaff Press Limited, 255A Upper Newtownards Road, Belfast BT4 3JF.

The cover illustration is reproduced from a sketchbook of J W Carey's by kind permission of Roger Weatherup.

ISBN 0 85640 099 8

Printed in Northern Ireland by Belfast Litho Printers Limited.

Contents

List of Illustrations

Foreword

Belfast has earned itself such a sad image in recent years that I would like to record some happier memories of what it was like to grow up in its outskirts soon after the first World War, and in particular my memories of one remarkable family.

Even when the Careys were living in Knock people would smilingly shake their heads and say someone really ought to write a book about them. But, of course, no one did. And now that they are no longer with us and that kindly, unhurried world in which they lived is just a memory I feel tempted to try, although I know I have no other qualifications than that I happened to be born into the house opposite theirs.

This book is about the Carey family, whose head was Joseph W. Carey, the artist and illustrator, but it is not intended as an appraisal of his work, although such a book could well be written. 'The Careys' had a way of looking at life, a humour and a humanity, which I and many others found very refreshing in this busy materialistic age, and it is in the hope that others who may not have known them may find them so too that I set down these memories.

I wish to acknowledge with gratitude the help given me by Alan Carey, Nelson Browne, Molly Greeves, Winston McCabe, Mrs Mackie, Ruth Parkes, Launcelot Turtle and my brother Morris Atkinson, all of whom have added their memories to mine; to Roger Weatherup for lending the sketchbook, and not least to my husband Oskar, without whose practical help and encouragement this book would never have seen the light of day.

Honor Rudnitzky

Brugh.

Part One

Brugh

1

Knock, where we all lived, was not a very remarkable place. It was a quiet, respectable middle-class neighbourhood, a place of tree-lined avenues and leafy lanes, where milk-floats clip-clopped on their rounds, the spokes of their wheels twinkling in the sunlight and Mr. Smart, the butcher in Ballyhackamore, who kept hackney ponies, delivered his wares in an elegant turn-out. Bread came round in enormous lurching bread-vans, drawn by what looked like cavalry chargers, and in the early morning on Fridays, before the trams started, you could hear the creaking rumble of country carts on the square setts of the Newtownards Road as they plodded in to market. The country was not far away then and every summer a corncrake came to the field behind our house.

Yet for all its sleepy tranquillity I think Knock must have produced more oddities to the square acre than any place else on earth. Not that the natives wished to appear odd or strike attitudes. They were individualists and perhaps in those days before the levelling influence of so much mass conformity it was easier to stay that way. There was also a sort of village solidarity amongst people who lived in Knock. For many years we were not bothered by new people moving in; it was not one of those rapidly developing areas, sought after by the socially ambitious, and people who lived there tended to stay. In fact, after the Second World War when housing was scarce, someone remarked on the number of daughters who, instead of moving away when they married, had brought their husbands home and were rearing their families in the houses in which they themselves had been born. 'Well,' as Arthur McCabe said who, having married Mary Carey, was one such, 'we all got very nice houses anyway.'

The houses of Knockdene Park did not conform to any overall plan, but rather reflected the individuality of Edwardian taste. There was a footpath on only one side of the road and separated from the road by a wide grass verge, planted with trees. The Careys' house had been designed by Mr. Carey himself and might have been dubbed 'quaint'. It was called 'Brugh', though why or what it means I regret I do not know, and it stood on a narrow triangle of garden where Knockdene Park divided itself, a pretty little archway of privet over each of its two entrances. It was not a large house yet it seemed to have many rooms and a great many doors because it was intended that Mr. Carey's aunt, Aunt Catharine Pasche, should live with them, and he had very prudently allocated her her own front door, living room and cooking arrangements. She had been born in Norway and was proud of the fact that in her youth she had refused the richest man in Bergen. She could speak seven languages, read the Bible in Hebrew and, like Mr. Carey, belonged to the Moravian Church.

Although I never knew her, I have been told that Aunt Catharine was a severely impressive-looking old lady in a lace cap, with strict ideas on tidiness, so perhaps it was as well that her apartment was virtually self-contained. She died a few years after coming to live with them at the age of eighty-nine, yet the house, for as long as the Careys lived in it, remained unaltered with its profusion of doors, passages and pantries.

There were three Carey children, Mary, Bruce and Alan who was my brother's friend and contemporary, but I was eight years younger than my brother, so that although I grew up with the Carey family the children were never my playmates, in fact, I cannot clearly remember Bruce before he had joined the Merchant Navy.

2

I cannot quite remember when I first became aware of the Careys, but I remember one day when I was riding my tricycle along the footpath, Mary, probably in her late teens, although she seemed very grown-up to me, came through the little privet archway and said: 'Would you like to see our kittens?'

Now you would think that anyone young enough to be riding a tricycle would jump at such an invitation, but not I. Already I had had unfortunate experiences with a well-meaning lady who had enticed me in and then plied me with milk and gingerbread, two things which I disliked. I therefore accepted invitations with caution, but in the case of the Careys there was a further confusion in my mind. 'Mr Carey' was also the name of the headmaster of my brother's prep. school, a person to be held in awe by all accounts, and I would have felt happier, had I known that Mr. Carey was not at home, but was too polite to ask such a question. Seeing me hesitate, Mary came across the road and took my hand. 'The naughty creature,' she said, 'she's had them in mother's Sunday hat.' So many of Morris's accounts of school escapades had ended with the words 'You ought to have heard what old man Carey had to say about that', that I felt I did not want to be anywhere around to hear what he might have to say about this. But Mary was already propelling me up the five steep steps to the front door, and a moment later had bundled me into what, for me, was a most wonderful room. Low ceilinged and rather dark, its walls were entirely covered with pictures.

I did not know then that Mr. Carey, far from being an awe-inspiring headmaster, was an artist with such a compassion for his fellow artists that he felt compelled to buy something whenever he went to an exhibition. His whole house was full of pictures, some good, some not so, but all enthralling to my young eyes. I remember one in particular, a large one opposite the door, depicting a fierce looking man in a white frilly skirt and embroidered waistcoat, waving murderous swords above his head as he whirled round in a dance, whilst other similarly dressed fierce men clapped him. I could not believe that anything so vivid and so exciting could only be a painting.

Mary, however, towed me past all these wonders and we disappeared through a wooden structure which I afterwards came to know as 'the Confessional'. It may have originally been designed to exclude draughts coming from the back regions, and as such it may have been moderately successful, but as an excluder of light entering these regions and the awkward stairs, which rose out of them, its success was total. We had nearly reached the top when a door opened and light flooded down.

'This is Betty,' said Mary, 'I've brought her over to see the kittens.'

'I don't think she's moved them yet,' Mr. Carey said vaguely.

He seemed to have a lot of frizzy grey hair about his head, bushy eyebrows, a walrus moustache and little tufts growing out of his ears, all rather alarming to a child, although on this first meeting I do not think my eyes went higher than his leggings. I did not know that when he went to his studio in Belfast he preferred to cycle, hence the leggings, and that he was seldom seen without them. In fact, he had even offended some aspiring Malone Road hostess by wearing them to her party.

Leggings were what our gardener wore. They were the excuse he made, when asked to come in and shift some heavy piece of furniture, for not coming further than the kitchen door. I felt that they ought not to be upstairs in a bedroom, not knowing that Mr. Carey used that room as a studio when he was at home. I felt that at any moment another door would open and some one would scold about the leggings for being where they were, the kittens for being where they were, and probably me for being there at all.

But Mr. Carey was already telling me, in his gentle, rather husky voice, of the habits of cats and how they normally moved their kittens after the first week. I gathered that the 'she' who had not removed them was not Mrs. Carey and that until the mother cat did so, Mrs. Carey would probably have to do without her Sunday hat.

3

What I did not know on that first meeting was that Mr. Carey was one of the best-known and most prolific of water-colour artists in Northern Ireland at the beginning of this century. I have been surprised to learn that he was born in 1850 so that by the time I came to know him he must have been nearly seventy. He was an excellent draughtsman and worked as an illustrator for the firm of Marcus Ward, as did his brother John. This firm employed a number of well known artists, such as Kate Greenaway and the Thomson brothers, of whom Hugh Thomson became very famous as an illustrator when he went to London. One of my personal treasures is an edition of Jane Austen, beautifully illustrated by him.

However, Marcus Ward failed in 1895 and after Mr. Carey had lost his savings, which he had unfortunately invested in the firm, he went into partnership with Dick Thomson, Hugh's brother, and continued to do the same sort of work in a top floor studio in Royal Avenue. Besides illustrating books, they did many illuminated addresses, which I should have thought would have been rather boring work. I have been looking at some of these addresses by Mr. Carey and there is nothing to suggest he found such work boring, in fact I have marvelled at the perfection of the little miniature scenes he put into them.

Possibly Mr. Carey took on too many commercial commissions, such as his series of Kelly's coal boats which appeared on calendars, and there are those who might say that that sort of thing could be better done by the camera. Yet no one could deny the delicacy of his detail or the sheer craftsmanship of his skies and backgrounds. It also speaks of his integrity that to the depicting of some small coasting vessel, setting out from harbour, he could bring all the skills which he brought to his other paintings so that they were not only an accurate record, but a pleasing scene as well. I have never seen any of his work that could be called slip-shod, and it is sad to reflect that someone who had spent a lifetime perfecting his technique in painting 'like real' should find his work superseded by the camera. Mr. Carey was truly a Victorian who happened to be living and painting in the 1920s in a manner no longer fashionable, but nonetheless not without its merit. Some day, when people tire of standing in front of a painting and wondering if the exhibitors have not made some mistake and hung it upside down, Mr. Carey's delicate exactitude may once again find its admirers.

Mr. Carey preferred his independence, and rather than submit to the vagaries of a Belfast tram he rode every day to the studio on his bicycle, carried it up all those flights of stairs and in the evening was to be seen, a familiar figure in his cape, pork-pie hat and leggings, steadily pushing his way up the long hill from the Holywood Arches with slow, deliberate thrusts of the pedals. I never heard him complain of the weather, the insolence of the increasing motor traffic or of even feeling tired, although it was not unknown for him to fall asleep at parties in the evening. Once an understanding hostess said: 'Just let him enjoy the party in his own way.'

Nevertheless, although he did sometimes drop off at frivolous gatherings, whilst playing chess he remained wide-awake, and my father, who was considered a better than average player, readily admitted that he was simply not in Mr. Carey's class. Mr. Carey belonged to the Shaftesbury Club and when, in about 1922, Capablanca, the then world champion, came to Belfast he engaged to play twenty-four games simultaneously in the Clarence Place Hall. He won twenty-two, and of the two that he lost, one was against a man from the shipyards who kept his cloth cap on throughout the encounter, and the other was Mr. Carey.

In his younger days he took an interest in ballooning which was never very successful here because the prevailing wind tended to blow the enthusiasts out to sea. He once described how, as they attempted to land, people could be seen running across the fields and jumping the ditches to try to keep up with the balloon, and how, when they threw down anchors, the men who caught the ropes were trailed over the ground. When they finally landed and were letting the gas out, some exhilarated spectator sought to relish the satisfaction of the moment by lighting his pipe! Fortunately Mr. Carey only lost his whiskers in the explosion, but after that the whole countryside was dotted with spectators fleeing for dear life back the way they had come.

Mr. Carey had a thing about dandelions. He could not bear to have them seed either in his own garden, in the Park or in anyone else's garden, and he believed, as I do, that the only way to get rid of them is by digging them out by the root. Armed with a special implement, he was sometimes discovered early in the morning on hands and knees on some neighbour's lawn, but by the time the household came down to breakfast this shy perfectionist had vanished, and only some little earthy pockmarks revealed the amount of good work that he had done. Once, during the troubles we had in 1922 when there was a curfew and the police were very vigilant because Sir James Craig, Northern Ireland's first Prime Minister, lived in Cabin Hill just at the end of Knockdene Park, Mr. Carey was apprehended at dusk one fine summer evening acting suspiciously but only to the peril of the dandelions.

4

Mrs. Carey was born in Scotland and first came to live at Knock as a governess to the three Misses Kelly. She was a very good watercolour painter too, in fact there are some who would say that of the two she was the better artist. Mr. Carey excelled at illustration, at little thumb-nail sketches where detail was all important, whereas Mrs. Carey with her bolder, more imprecise style was very successful at capturing the atmosphere of the Irish scene, with its dark mountains, lowering rain clouds and bogs. If Mr. Carey had a fault, it was that he sometimes worked over his bigger paintings in too much detail. Recognising this, Mrs. Carey would hide them from him to stop him doing anything more to them, and it was not unknown to find a painting stuffed down behind the piano.

Mrs. Carey was a busy bustling little figure, always dressed in black with a little bit of lace at her neck and a touch of blue about her somewhere, either a brooch, a scarf or a ribbon in her hat. Her hats were always of the same, rather squashed shape, which she wore straight on her head in the manner of Mrs. Noah, ignoring the current trend for close fitting cloches. She was a Presbyterian, a fervent teetotaller and a staunch supporter of the Unionist Party. My father was none of these things, except possibly the latter at election time, and when he knew anyone had strongly held views he could never resist the temptation of 'trailing his coat.' A mischievous twinkle would come into his eye and we would slip something provocative into the conversation. Mrs. Carey rose like a bird every time, and many and wide-ranging were the arguments they held, ending usually with one or the other walking down the garden path sadly shaking their head over the wrong-headedness of the other. But they never became bitter, and when again they met they would laughingly refer to the differences they had had before, which quite often started them off all over again.

Mrs. Carey painted anything she thought might be improved by a little colour, happily daubing a flower here or there on any empty space which offended her eye, or on the faded parts of the cretonne covers, which resulted in several visitors acquiring pansy pants. When faced with misfortunes of this kind, she had a most disarming smile and a habit of scuttling from one room to another, leaving sentences and much else unfinished behind her. Once, when they had a cottage in the Mournes, she painted the kitchen chairs green, and then on the seat of each a bouquet of flowers, after which they all went out sketching. Mr. Carey, arriving on a later bus and toiling up the mountainside with everything that everyone else had forgotten, flopped exhausted on the first chair he found and fell asleep. Later, when roused and made aware of the disaster, he just said: 'They must have been far too distinct before, so I've toned them down a bit.'

5

Because of its position between two branches of Knockdene Park the Careys allowed their friends and neighbours to make a short cut through their garden. The house, therefore, became a centre for casual callers who dropped in at any hour of the day or night to exchange some titbit of gossip and were always made welcome. The Careys never seemed to mind this invasion of their privacy. Even late at night people, returning from some controversial play or film, would drop in to the Careys to air their views about it, and arguments were often pursued until a late hour, unless it happened to be a Saturday night, when Mrs. Carey, as a daughter of the Manse, would intervene to point out that it was already the Sabbath, a day of peace and rest, and time that everyone went home.

Percy French was a great friend of the Careys and a frequent visitor. He used to arrive unannounced, saying: 'Did you get my telegram? — No? — Well, here it is in my pocket!'

In many ways he and Mr. Carey had much in common. Neither had a head for business and both were amateurs in the true sense of the word, in that they did what they did for the sheer love of doing it, and the fact that they earned money thereby was just an accidental bonus.

When he arrived Percy French would insist on having what he called 'a gathering of the clans' at which everyone would either sing or draw sketches, and although at the time these parties were taking place I was still being pushed around in my pram, they bore a similarity to the parties I later enjoyed. In the seventeenth century, if you went to a party, your education was expected to be such that if you were handed a piece of music you could sight-read your part in a madrigal. If you could not sight-read, or worse, could not sing I imagine the evening must have been painful indeed, and I expect you were never asked back, but at the Carey's parties, whether you could draw or not, you were simply handed a piece of paper and a pencil. If you could draw your efforts were applauded; if not, they only added to the hilarity of the evening.

William Conor was one whose efforts at the writing games benefitted by this indulgence. Of course, as an artist he could acquit himself, but at the other pencil-and-paper games he did not shine.

Most people think of Percy French as the man who wrote 'The Mountains of Mourne' and forget that he was also a well-known watercolour artist and concert party entertainer. During the First World War he travelled all over Ireland, which was all one in those days, entertaining the troops and raising money for the Red Cross. He turned his artistic abilities to doing 'turns' on the stage. He would do a lightning sketch which looked pleasing enough when presented to the audience, but when turned upside down would be shown to represent something quite different. Another of his 'stunts' would be to hold a plain white plate over a candle until it became black and then with the reverse end of a paintbrush etch in a little scene. These plates could be hung on a wall, and I believe there are still some in existence. He did these things just as readily and with just as much zest at a Carey party as he did on the stage, and because he enjoyed telling stories and making people laugh he was always the life and soul of the party. The evening usually ended with him singing some of his own songs.

By contrast Mr. Carey was much too shy and retiring to take the centre of the floor, but when it came to the drawing games he came into his own. They both were just as happy to perform for their friends for nothing as they were to please their public professionally.

Percy French enjoyed children and had no objection to having them round him whilst he worked. Once, when Bruce, Alan and Morris were watching him, he suddenly turned to them and said: 'Well, what do you think of it?' Alan and Morris were too dumbfounded to say anything, but Bruce, who was older, plucked up courage and said: 'I think the foreground isn't right. The purple of the heather is too strong.' A short, but dreadful silence followed. Then Percy French said: 'The boy's right,' and wiped out the foreground.

The 1910 Sketching Club which took its name from the date of its foundation was formed by a Miss Jones. Its members submitted a sketch each quarter to be criticized by the others, and although I have no evidence that Percy French influenced its foundation it is true that he formed a similar club many years earlier when he was working in Cavan.

Miss Jones had taught my mother and although my mother was not a member of the club she was always interested in it, and we were often able to intercept the folio as it went on its rounds and pore over its contents. Possibly because of his professional standing, but more probably because of pressure of work, Mr. Carey did not contribute sketches, but he joined in the criticism and his remarks were always helpful and constructive. Sometimes he would do a little drawing in the margin to suggest how a composition might be improved. The club had a healthy membership and continued to function until after the Second World War.

But there were some drawbacks in having Percy French staying in the house. Pulling a wry face, Mrs. Carey confided to my mother: 'He's just wiped his brushes on the new spare-room wallpaper.'

6

I doubt if the Careys ever bothered to lock their front door. And it was not really necessary because it had become so warped that it was impossible to open, either smoothly or silently, without making the knocker hiccough violently. 'Is that you, dear?' would come Mrs. Carey's voice from somewhere, and even if you were not the 'dear' she had been expecting she always seemed delighted that you had come.

Once, hearing a noise in the middle of the night, she came downstairs to find two policemen having a cup of tea in the kitchen. This pleased her temperance principles so much that she was not in the least annoyed and warmly invited them to drop in any time when passing on their beat.

She was interested in numerous good causes and often promised quantities of things for sales of work, but then forgot the date for which they should be ready so that frequent crises occurred, when the whole family and anyone else who happened to be passing would be pressed into finishing some urgent consignment. Often, when I had squeezed myself round the grudging front door, I would be greeted with 'Betty, dear, just go on with this whilst I go and see if the fish has come,' and some strange employment would be placed in my unskilled hands. Sometimes we would be madly dotting flowers on Woolworth toothmugs — 'mother's promised three dozen of these for to-morrow' — or decorating matchboxes or brooches with swirls of sealing wax, or lacquering and threading strings of curiously shaped beads, previously made by rolling up strips of glued brown paper. At one time, I remember, we went through a phase of decorating crockery, but that was not always a success because the tubes of special paint, which had afterwards to be fired, kept on getting confused with the tubes of ordinary paint with which the house abounded. The designs sometimes came back to us with bits missing so that the flowers had yellow centres and green leaves, but no petals, and other such mishaps.

There were also the posters, advertising these events, and although neither my spelling nor my lettering were reliable, I was let loose on these too. Once when the double 'a' in bazaar turned up in the wrong place Mrs. Carey just said it was a funny-looking word either way. Whether the organizers of the sale thought the same, or what kind of people ever bought the things we made were happily questions that never entered my head.

Nowadays, when I look at the work of abstract artists, I sometimes feel that Mrs. Carey and I were before our time. The effects of splodges of paint, trickling this way and that, which these artists obtain by studiously tilting their canvases hither and thither, happened with us only too naturally, and some of our most remarkable designs in sealing wax were obtained by trying to remove pickles of bird seed from them.

Once the bazaar was held in the Careys' house and, peeping out of our side gate, I saw with enormous pride that my poster was propped up against their hedge. There was a tremendous commotion of ladies coming and going. Suddenly Mrs. Carey came out, scurried up the path into our house and, flopping into a chair, lay with her eyes closed. My mother thought she had probably come over to borrow something, but had forgotten what.

'You must be very busy in your house this morning,' she ventured, attempting to bring her back to the realities of the moment.

'The whole Park is in our house, arranging everything,' said Mrs. Carey, 'so I just thought I'd slip over here for a few minutes' peace, until they have got it settled.'

Later that afternoon I heard Mrs. Carey calling for silence because Mrs. McAleery (afterwards better known on the wireless as Mrs. Rooney) was about to give one of her recitations. In those days children were taught elocution and although I did not care much for the subject I stood outside the door and listened eagerly enough to hear how a grown-up would do it. When I heard her begin with her inimitable 'Friends dears and neighbours all' I was so flabbergasted I hardly knew where to look. That any lady should stand up in Mrs. Carey's drawing room and declaim to the company in the exact tones and accents of our charwoman I found amazing, and I was even more amazed that all the other ladies should find it so amusing and should clap so delightedly when she finished.

In after years, of course, I came to appreciate 'Mrs. Rooney' very much indeed, but at the age of about seven I think I must have been a horrid little snob.

7

I think the Careys were the first people in Knockdene Park to have a wireless, a small crystal set encased in an ugly box with two sets of headphones. After Mary had twiddled the cat's whisker to get a good reception we would sit round the table tethered to this magical box. Mrs. Carey was usually the one who, getting up suddenly, would forget she was tethered. 'I don't know why they ever called it wire*less*,' she said after jerking the whole contraption on to the floor. Today's children, who treat moon walks as so much background noise, would have been amazed to see us sitting there enraptured, holding one earphone each to our ears, which was what we had to do if more than two wished to listen. In that way I listened to many Children's Hours.

Then one day when I was not there Mary heard it announced that there would be a competition for the best illustration of some story which was then read, and decided that I should enter. The story as re-told to me by Mary was not really very inspiring, in fact it was rather confused and hard to follow, but anyhow I tried to oblige though without much heart, and Mary posted it off. She was disappointed when some other child was announced as the winner, but I cannot say that I was as it had not been my idea in the beginning. All competitors were invited to the studio where the entries would be displayed and Mary, my mother and I set off.

The Belfast station then operated from a building in Linenhall Street, somewhere behind where the present B.B.C. building now stands and we had to climb a great many stairs to reach the studio. Once inside Mary set up such a lamentation about her stupidity in not realizing that the illustrations were to be painted, and she kept on apologizing all the way home in the tram, which was quite unnecessary. I was quite happy that my unsuccessful entry had allowed me to see round the studio.

All the aunts and uncles whose voices we knew were all there showing people round, answering questions and making themselves agreeable. The studio had a very thick carpet and heavy curtains to deaden the sound they said, and the microphones were slung on thick mats of sponge rubber to absorb any vibration. One uncle told us that each mike cost £300 (a vast sum to me) and could be disrupted by a simple sneeze. Whether this was really so or whether it was just this uncle's way of protecting the mike from inquisitive children I do not know, but I, who was subject to hay fever, was so impressed that I could hardly breathe in or out until we were safely outside in the street again.

Soon after this my aunt and uncle, who also lived in Knockdene Park, bought a wireless set, but theirs was a very grand affair, a valve set, which did without earphones. It was housed in a coffinlike chest with a lid which lifted up to reveal an array of knobs and dials. My uncle would stand in front of it, adjust his spectacles, flex his arms to shorten his cuffs as if he were about to address the Sunday joint, and then begin the process of 'tuning in'. The machine made the most dreadful squeals and squawks.

'Those are just the waves,' explained my aunt, then seeing my astonished face, 'the sound waves, I mean, not the sea.'

Like many other little girls at that time I attended Miss Nairn's dancing class and she hired the Ulster Hall for her end of term display. Someone, probably my father, had told me that Mr. Carey had done the murals, now sadly murky, and as my class were engaged in showing the assembled doting mums, grannies and nannies how we could point our toes and turn ourselves about, I suddenly looked up and saw the paintings. Thereafter I lost interest in the class's performance and stood gazing upward after they had all finished and gone, and some harassed assistant teacher rushed out to tow me away.

'What on earth were you doing out there all by yourself?' flustered my mother.

'I was looking at Mr. Carey's paintings,' I said, which to me seemed a perfectly reasonable thing to do, albeit in the middle of a dancing display, but it did not make me either Miss Nairn's favourite pupil nor my mother's pride and joy.

At the far end of the Carey's garden, beside the big lilac, there stood a summerhouse, a faded erection, wanly white, smelling of damp and overrun with spiders. It was here that Mary once discovered a tramp dossing down for the night but instead of being frightened or annoyed she cooked him a herring for his breakfast and brought it out to him, and it was here that one summer Mary chose to hold a spasmodic painting class for me and others of my age. The instruction was neither given nor received very seriously, in fact my clearest memories of those afternoons were of Mary's dreamy voice reciting from memory long passages of Edward Lear.

Mr. Carey sometimes came out to see how we were getting on. Once he found me exasperated with a house which, as I put it, 'wouldn't go sideways into my picture'. He sat down and explained perspective to me, and soon I was happily projecting railway lines with telegraph wires or corridors with chequered tiling into infinity. These exercises may have been of doubtful artistic merit, much frowned upon by those who believe that children should be left to express their views of things as best they may, but to me, at any rate, they afforded great satisfaction.

Mr. Carey had a wonderful store of knowledge on many subjects and a habit of saying the most interesting things in such a diffident, barely audible way that you had to listen intently if you were not to miss something. He knew a great deal about local history and he passed on what he knew of these things and of the technique of drawing and painting as if you were a grown-up who shared his interests. He never made me feel I was being talked down to, yet he took infinite pains to explain. He knew a lot about sailing and ships and how they were rigged, and had a withering contempt for artists who put blobs all over the rigging, suggesting pulley blocks, without understanding how blocks were used and sails raised.

I remember, when I was older, going with a school friend to ask his advice about period costume. Our school was producing a pageant on the history of Belfast and we wanted to know if in 1613 when Belfast got its charter our characters ought to be wearing the Elizabethan ruff or already the pointed lace collar of the Stuarts. Far from being annoyed at having his Saturday afternoon disturbed, Mr. Carey's blue eyes twinkled and, trotting upstairs to his studio, returned laden with folios which he and his brother had compiled

'Perspective drawing' from J. W. Carey's sketchbook.

on period costume. We sat together on the window seat in the hall, whilst he spread them before us, explaining all the while. Where he could not find an illustration for some particular fashion he supplied it on the spot with one of his meticulous little thumbnail sketches. We were treated to a great deal more than the fashions of Belfast in 1613.

As he turned the pages of the folios he came upon a pound note, nestling between the drawings. 'I wonder how that got there,' he said and, slipping it unconcernedly into his pocket, went on talking about the things in life which really interested him.

I think we traced the whole development of design in lace from its beginnings in Flanders to its establishment in Ireland, with digressions into the coming of the Huguenots and the beginning of linen in Ireland. I remember we came across an illustration of a galleon and he told us of how one, supposedly containing the Armada's treasure, had sunk in Tobermorey Bay. He would have been enormously excited by the recovery of the Girona's treasure, and in fact in a sketch book recently loaned to me I find that he pasted in a reproduction of a painting he did of a galleon being wrecked at Port-na-Spania. He writes that the picture was painted for the Belfast Art Society's Exhibition in 1895 and subsequently bought by Mr. Robert Day of Cork. It is not such a dramatic smash-up as that depicted on the leaflet 'Girona 1972', produced by the Ulster Museum, and better conveys the ponderous weight of a stricken, water-logged vessel nearing her end. Mr. Carey states that he painted a similar picture which was destroyed when the Royal Hibernian Academy was burnt in Dublin in 1916, but that he re-painted it for the purchaser, Mr. Orpen. He states, however, that the Girona was wrecked at Bush Bay and that an unidentified ship foundered at Port-na-Spania, which was the popular belief until the discoveries at Port-na-Spania proved otherwise.

It is interesting that the scene of such a disaster is called Port-na-Spania in the North of Ireland, whereas a similar location in Co. Clare in Eire is called Spanish Point. My father, who always liked to hear the local version of events, once asked an old fisherman we met there how Spanish Point got its name.

'Well,' said the old man, 'about sixty years ago, or maybe more — I mind me grandfather telling of it — a Spanish man-of-war drove ashore here and was lost with all hands, and they called her "The Armada".'

Mr. Carey was engaged to give private painting lessons to some young ladies in 1930, and the sketch book I have mentioned was compiled by him as a text book for his lessons, freely illustrating the points he wished to make, and imparting a great deal else on many subjects of general interest. He begins by sorting out the paints into two columns, headed 'Sheep' and 'Goats', those which were permanent and those which faded, dismissing Sap Green with the advice 'throw it away'. His experience had taught him to use colours which lasted, and all the paintings are as fresh as on the day he did them. Of course there are several pages about boats and the effect of the changing whether on skies and seas and, as always, he imparts a great deal of knowledge on general topics. Through it all his humour keeps on popping out as, under a pleasing little scene showing the advantage of concentrating interest at one point, he writes 'Dissipation weakens pictures (and artists)' and again 'Figures should normally be very quiet and restful... and a curve in the back, such as you find in gardeners employed by the week is very suitable.' Altogether it is a treasure of a book and all the more to be marvelled at by having been put together by an old gentleman in his eightieth year.

9

During the First World War Mrs. Carey had been the official Red Cross visitor to all the War Hospitals in Belfast. She was always eager to help people, and when she was made a Justice of the Peace in 1921 she took a great interest in the women and children who appeared in the Petty Sessions' Courts before her, often following up their cases and befriending them by having them to her home. She sometimes tried to help them by offering a few hours' cleaning in the house, or tidying up the garden to some of their husbands. Then one day some family miniatures disappeared. They were charming little portraits of gentlemen with Regency sideburns in high collared velvet coats, some of them painted on ivory, and probably quite valuable. 'Not at all the sort of thing that Mrs. So-and-so would lift,' said Mrs. Carey. Nevertheless an air of doubt and distrust overshadowed the house, until it was noticed that the mantelpiece in the morning room was beginning to part from the

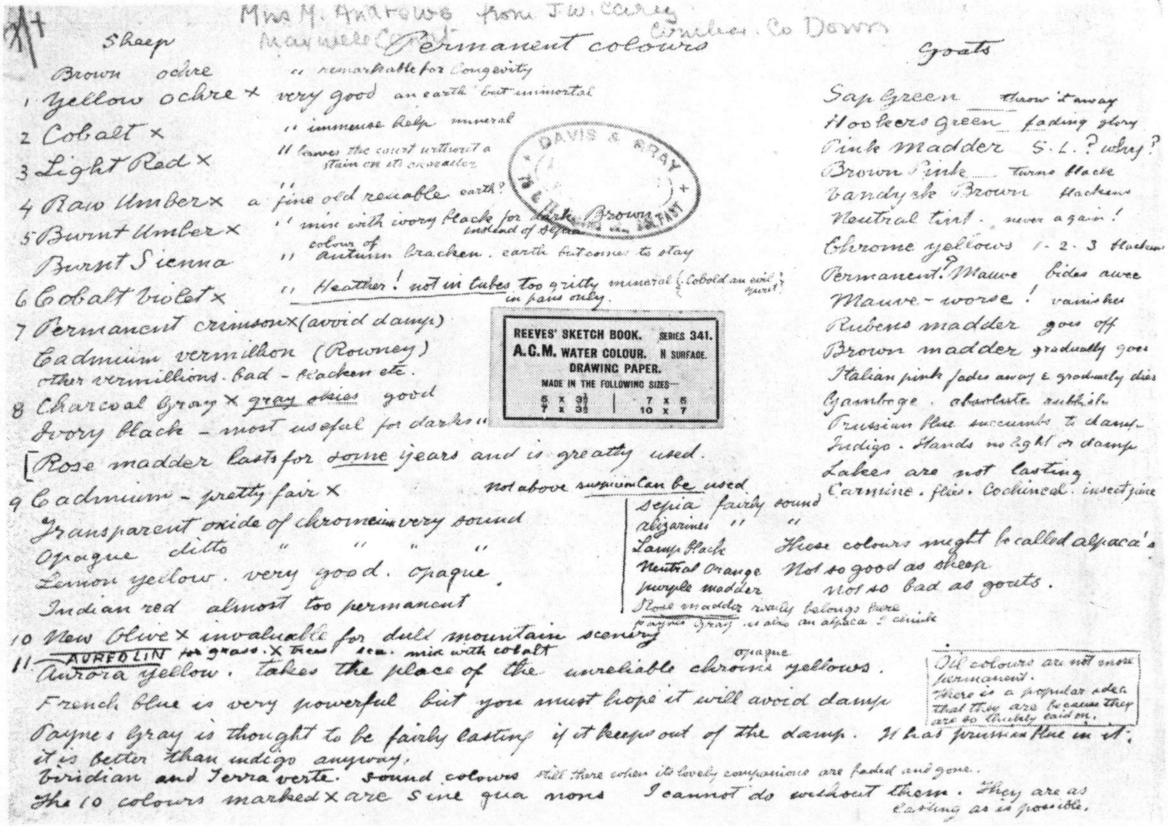

Miss M. Andrews from J. W. Carey
Maxwell Court Comber. Co Down

Permanent colours

Sheep

Brown ochre " remarkable for longevity
1 Yellow ochre × very good an earth but immortal
2 Cobalt × " immense help mineral
3 Light Red × " leaves the court without a stain on its character
4 Raw Umber × a fine old reliable earth?
5 Burnt Umber × " mix with ivory black for dark Brown instead of Sepia
Burnt Sienna " colour of autumn bracken. earth but comes to stay
6 Cobalt violet × " Heather! not in tubes too gritty mineral in pans only
7 Permanent crimson × (avoid damp)
Cadmium vermillion (Rowney)
other vermillions. bad - blacken etc.
8 Charcoal Gray × gray skies good
Ivory black - most useful for darks "
[Rose madder lasts for some years and is greatly used.
9 Cadmium - pretty fair × Not above can be used
Transparent oxide of chromium very sound
Opaque ditto " " " "
Lemon yellow. very good. opaque.
Indian red almost too permanent
10 New Olive × invaluable for dull mountain scenery
11 AUREOLIN for grass. × trees mix with cobalt
Aurora yellow. takes the place of the unreliable chrome yellows. opaque
French blue is very powerful but you must hope it will avoid damp
Paynes Gray is thought to be fairly lasting if it keeps out of the damp. It has prussian blue in it.
it is better than indigo anyway.
Viridian and Terra verte. sound colours still there when its lovely companions are faded and gone.
The 10 colours marked × are sine qua nons I cannot do without them. They are as lasting as is possible.

Sepia fairly sound
Alizarines " "
Lamp black These colours might be called alpaca's
Neutral Orange Not so good as sheep
purple madder not so bad as goats.
Rose madder really belongs here
Paynes Gray is also an alpaca I think

Goats

Sap Green throw it away
Hookers green fading glory
Pink madder S.L.? why?
Brown Pink turns black
Vandyke Brown blackens
Neutral tint. never again!
Chrome yellows 1. 2. 3 blacken
Permanent? Mauve fides awee
Mauve - worse! vanishes
Rubens madder goes off
Brown madder gradually goes
Italian pink fades away & gradually dies
Gamboge. absolute rubbish
Prussian blue succumbs to damp
Indigo. Stands no light or damp
Lakes are not lasting
Carmine. flies. Cochineal insect juice

Oil colours are not more permanent.
There is a popular idea that they are because they are so thickly laid on.

DAVIS & GRAY BELFAST

REEVES' SKETCH BOOK. SERIES 341.
A.C.M. WATER COLOUR. N SURFACE.
DRAWING PAPER.
MADE IN THE FOLLOWING SIZES—
5 x 3½ | 7 x 5
7 x 3½ | 10 x 7

'Sheep and goats' from J. W. Carey's sketchbook.

wall. When the reason for this was investigated, the miniatures came to light and everyone was happy again.

As the depression developed and unemployment became widespread, Mrs. Carey helped in a soup kitchen in Ballymacarrett, and long before youth clubs were heard of, Mary was running clubs there. They produced a pantomime, usually written by Mary, every Christmas, and my party slippers would be loaned to Cinderella. My mother and I were invited to the performance which was held in the clubrooms, somewhere off Dee Street.

In the summer the tranquillity of Knockdene Park would be shattered when Mary would invite a whole group to play in the garden. Once one of the boys fell out of a tree and broke his arm. Mary rushed him to hospital and the nurse asked her to wait while it was being x-rayed.

'But I can't,' said Mary, 'I've left eleven of them running wild at home.'

The nurse looked at her severely. 'You don't mean to tell me,' she said, 'that you are the mother of twelve.'

With Mrs. Carey concerned with her magisterial duties and all her other committees and meetings and Mary with her interests, Mr. Carey would frequently come home to an empty house. If someone had left him something to eat, he ate it, if not, he went uncomplainingly upstairs to his studio, and if asked later whether he had had anything to eat, he would say: 'I think so. What's this it was?' He hardly seemed to notice what he ate.

Once, on the way home after a pleasant evening, Mrs. Carey remarked to him how kind it was of their hostess to give him his favourite dinner — roast duck and green peas — and he said: 'Was that what it was? Och, why didn't you tell me?'

Both Mary and her father loved to share the pleasure they got from drawing and painting with others, and I remember years afterwards, when I had left school, Mary roped me in to help her with a class she was running for the boys of Malone Training School. The then principal of the school wanted the boys to have some more varied interests and I sometimes thought their interest in our art class was not unconnected with the bag of sweets Mary brought with her each week. Certainly, like those earlier classes in the summerhouse, they were light-hearted breaks in the strict routine of reformatory life, and I doubt if the boys learnt very much about art, although I learnt a lot about how not to teach it. The boys were always most anxious to please, but the trouble was they interpreted me literally. When I said: 'Don't bother with the eyes and eyebrows at this stage — just draw a shape for the head — doesn't matter what it looks like — a football or a turnip — you can do the details later —' that was precisely what I got next week.

But I am running too far ahead in time..

10

As the depression grew worse Alan Carey left for America. Bruce had already been at sea for some years, and it was about this time that he brought back a parrot in the traditional manner, a wicked-eyed bird called Lorita. She was supposed to be capable of being trained to speak, but never justified this supposition. In true Carey manner she was not confined to a cage, but was allowed the run of the morning room. Large branches were erected for her in the bay window and newspapers were spread on the floor, but so far as I could see the newspapers were the only things that escaped damage, and Lorita became one more reason for careful circumspection before taking a seat. I never really cared for Lorita.

However, Mrs. Carey persisted, with much patience and many sugar lumps, in trying to get this dreadful bird to say 'Alan', with the result that when anyone entered the room all conversation was made impossible by its screeching 'Aha, Aha.' Mrs. Carey maintained that the 'dear bird', as she called her, was trying to say 'Alan', and spurned the suggestion that it was simply blackmail for more sugar, which was the only way silence could be bought.

Mary had some idea that Lorita could be taught to speak by rattling the poker in the grate. This certainly stimulated the bird, but only to make more frightful screeches.

Some time after this the Careys invested in a beautiful grey Persian cat, Angela, and announced that they were going to breed pure Persians and sell them for enormous sums. It was the sort project which I thought might get out of hand with the Careys, and I was right, for to this day there is about the cats of Knock, even down to the commonest tabby and marmalade, a certain Persian fleeciness.

There was no denying that Angela was a real beauty. She raised my hopes that Lorita's days might be numbered, but instead it was

Angela who was overawed. She preferred to sun herself in the bay window of the hall and watch everything that passed in the Park.

Possibly missing Alan, Mrs. Carey persuaded Bruce to leave the Merchant Navy and come home, which was unfortunate. She explained that she thought life at sea was not good for his 'health', but the frustrations of looking for and then holding down some uncongenial job during the 1930s in Belfast did nothing to improve his 'health'.

He bought himself a car which even at that time was considered to belong to the old crock class. It was one of those upright two-seater machines, nowadays fashionable as designs on ashtrays, with a dickey seat at the back and a canvas hood jutting forward, giving it a surprised expression. It only had one door on the passenger side and no self-starter, and once Bruce parked it in Donegall Place and switched off the engine before he noticed that the only door was against a lamp post. In the end some kindly passer-by responded to his imploring tappings on the cellophane window and pushed him forward so that he could get out.

Arthur McCabe also specialized in elderly cars which would never have passed a test for roadworthiness. Yet possibly because there were fewer cars about at that time or possibly because some guardian angel looked after him, he never had any serious accident and was able to do things which would have been fatal for any ordinary mortal. Once he took Mary and others for a drive one evening in a car which had no self-starter and whose brakes were almost non-existent, so that the only way of braking was by changing to a lower gear. Just as he was about to do this at the top of Ballymiscaw he missed his change and the engine stalled. From then on they mounted the bank round every hair-pin bend, but fortunately met nothing trying to come up the hill. When they finally trundled to a halt somewhere on the Belmont Road, Arthur said he thought his passengers looked a little green.

Bruce struggled along with various uninteresting jobs and from time to time his 'health' as his mother called it, suffered relapses. He tried hard to keep these lapses from his mother's notice, but eventually he lost his licence. He explained to her that he found the car too expensive to run and that he was laying it up for six months.

However, a policeman called at the house, explaining that he had come about Mr. Carey losing his licence.

'Oh well,' said Mrs. Carey, 'I'm sure it will turn up somewhere.'

They continued to talk at cross-purposes, with Mrs. Carey assuring the man that she would keep a look out for it when dusting.

'No, ma'am,' said the policeman, 'he lost it in the courts.'

'Oh well then,' said Mrs. Carey, 'it's sure to turn up. I am a J.P., you know, and they know me very well down there, so anyone finding it is sure to hand it in.'

When eventually truth dawned, poor Mrs. Carey was very grieved. Yet it was not long before, on looking back over the conversation she had had with the policeman, her little titter broke out and she was unable to keep her amusement to herself.

11

I have already mentioned the shape of the Carey's garden with the two gateways on either side, and their kindness in allowing us and others to use the short cut. Uninvited, errand boys on their bicycles used it too, and Mrs. Carey would in vain rap on the window, brandishing a paint brush or a toasting fork or anything else she happened to have in her hand at the time. One of these boys worked for a grocer called Love and Mrs. Carey called him Cupid because he was the messenger of Love.

At length someone pointed out if they continued to allow people to use the short cut it would become a right of way, and that to prevent this they must erect gates. This suggestion brought forth many more regarding the design of the gates. Everyone made suggestions and many even made drawings.

Mrs. Carey was hard to please. She did not want anything too solid, nor suburban, nor yet too ornamented, a plain barred gate was too farm-like, a solid one too prison-like. Meantime, the errand boys continued to skim through like minnows, and I began to think that the right of way would be established long before a design for a suitable gate had been selected. It probably would have been, too, had things not been brought to a head by old Mr. Osborne being knocked down by one of the boys as he shot out on to the road. Mr. Osborne had long been a centre of interest to us as children because it was rumoured that he wore a wig. We used to shadow him, furtively peeping up at the curious way his gingerbrown hair jutted out over the back of his collar. Yet when the naked truth lay revealed before our eyes there was only a feeling of horror. Mrs. Carey too seemed more outraged that the wig had been knocked off than that the old gentleman had been knocked down. Such things must not happen, and gates would be erected forthwith.

Some people may have thought that earlier on when I said that Knock seemed to have more eccentrics to the square acre than any place else on earth I was exaggerating, but this Mr. Osborne and his brother would help to substantiate my statement. They were both bald from childhood, and one wrote little 'poems' which he pushed under the Careys' doormat, touching renderings such as:

'There is a hill, called Scrabo Hill,
That hides my love from me.
I'll bore a hole through Scrabo Hill
That I my love may see.'

The other brother insisted on singing at the Careys' parties, and Alan once brightened the evening for old Mr. Steele, who was stone-deaf, by slipping him a note which said: 'Blessed are the deaf for they shall be spared.'

After all the artistic controversy about the design of the gates, what finally appeared, needless to say, satisfied no-one. They were flimsy structures roughly in the form of a Union Jack, kept closed by such a powerful spring that they only opened under squealing protest and slammed shut again as if they must shatter themselves to smithereens. Only the agile managed to get through unscathed.

The end of one of the gates came not long afterwards when the grocer's van demolished it. The driver maintained that the van's steering failed, although I wondered if he had not been waving good-bye to one of the maids. Anyhow, be that as it may, the van went in one bound from our back steps across the road and arrived on the Careys' lawn with the fragments of the gate festooning its bonnet. Mary and her mother rushed out of the house. When facing disaster, Mary had a habit of silently placing her hand along one cheek and closing both her eyes for several moments. When she opened them again she said to the man in her gentle voice: 'Would you like a cup of tea?', which seemed to unnerve the poor man more than the accident.

The other gate continued to irritate the neighbourhood with its squeals and bangs for many long years until finally old age overtook its timbers, though never its vehement spring.

Mrs. Carey could extricate herself from almost any predicament with her little deprecating titter. She and the late Lady Clanwilliam had become friendly through their association in various women's organizations, but when visiting Montalto, Mrs. Carey always seemed to have the most calamitous experiences with the butler, as when, on being helped into her coat she went down the lining and had to come out and begin again, or when, having decided to tip the man five shillings, she carefully put two half crowns into one pocket and transferred two pennies into another, only to find on her way down the drive that she still had the two half crowns with her. Whether or not her little titter worked its charm the next time she met the butler is not related.

Someone who was present at an annual dinner of one of these women's organizations held in Thompson's restaurant told me she was pleased to see Mrs. Carey's name in the place beside her. However, the dinner began and had reached the fish course before Mrs. Carey appeared. She was wearing, for her, a rather décolleté black satin evening dress, her inevitable black stockings, and was swathed about with a somewhat pearl-white lace shawl. She carried a large basket of pungent vegetables and a pair of lorgnettes. A subsequent press report of the proceedings stated that Mrs. Carey made the speech of the evening, wearing a black satin gown, veiled with lace. The vegetables, apparently, beggared description.

Holding the gaze of the startled company at bay with the lorgnettes, she made her way up the room to Lady Clanwilliam to whom she made her apologies, explaining the vegetables as purchases made at a Unionist bazaar at which she had been helping all day, so she had not had time to go home.

This done, she went to her place and put the reeking celery under the table as if there was nothing in the world more natural to do at a formal dinner, then greeted her friends on either hand and settled composedly to her dinner. Only when attention was no longer focussed upon her did she confide to her neighbour with a suppressed giggle: 'I made rather a mistake this evening. To begin with, I thought we were holding this dinner in the Carlton. I knew I would not have time to go home after the bazaar, so I packed a bag and went to the Carlton to change. I found I had forgotten to put in my dress — you'd never know this is my petticoat, would you? — and so I just asked Miss Henry if I might have the loan of one of the lace curtains out of the ladies' room.'

Jan 6. 1922

Magazine

People we Know.

MRS. J. W. CAREY, J.P.

Mrs. Carey, wife of J. W. Carey, the well-known water colour artist, is a daughter of the Rev. W. J. Fisher, of Aberlemno, Forfarshire, whose ancestors were for generations ministers of that parish, and it is interesting to know that some of them fought at Culloden for the Stewart's lost cause.

Everyone knows what valuable work was done by Mrs. Carey, both during the war and since then. She was Colonial Red Cross Visitor for all Belfast Hospitals during the war, and is the only official Red Cross Visitor at Victoria Barracks' Hospital.

Mrs. Carey was also greatly interested in buffet work for sailors and soldiers; indeed her interests are many, being a Member of Committee for the Women's Legion Gold Embroidery Workshops, and of the Central Committee of Women's Training, which has given many grants for training to women who have suffered from the effects of the war, and for many years she has been a Member of the Ulster Women's Unionist Council and Executive Committee.

In January, 1921, Mrs. Carey was made a Magistrate, and is deeply interested in the women and children who appear in the Petty Sessions' Courts.

As an artist Mr. Carey is well known throughout Ulster, and Mrs. Carey is equally well known and highly thought of for her sunny disposition and willingness to help in any good cause which will benefit the

A press report about Mrs. Carey.

Few people indeed could make the speech of the evening, swathed in a curtain from the ladies' room. Few, when faced with such a predicament, would have the courage or the resourcefulness even to try, but only Mrs. Carey, who had fortunately packed the lorgnettes, could carry it off with charm and dignity.

12

Mary was frequently scribbling, and it was rumoured that she was writing a book, but so far as I know it was never finished. She, who was such a delight to talk to, whose descriptions of everyday things were always so fresh and spontaneous, became sadly inhibited when she came to write them down. Years later she wrote accounts of the sailing trips she made, but they read strangely flat compared to her verbal accounts of these same adventures. Only in her letters did she write as she talked.

A letter from the Careys was always something which brightened the day. Mary usually began it in her rambling way, making ordinary every day events sound like amusing adventures, then other members of the family gave their versions and finally Mr. Carey added his, often in the form of a little sketch in the margin, which gave a quite different interpretation to the text. He treated a novel by Amanda McKittrick Ros in the same way. She was a lady of literary aspirations, the wife of the stationmaster in Larne, who without any very intimate knowledge of Edwardian high society wrote about it in a richly flamboyant style, well larded with alliteration and freely splashed about with mixed metaphors and ambiguous adjectives. Mrs. Carey, who visited her, maintained with some truth that she had a wonderful talent for words, but Mr. Carey's delicate little commentaries in the margin illustrated only too devastatingly the perils of such a gift.

I remember once getting a letter from Mary in which in the confines of one paragraph she related how Angela that morning had found a mouse drowned in the milk, how she lifted it out and licked it all over just as the St. Bernard dogs do to people buried in the snow; how Mr. Greeves had called to see the dogs at the monastery during his recent travels; how cool it had been in the mountains in contrast to Florence where it was so hot he had taken off his jacket in the Uffizi and had at once got into trouble with the attendants for being improperly dressed. Few people nowadays bother to use paragraphs in their letters, but there must be few indeed who could so smoothly glide from a mouse in the milk to poor Mr. Greeves' embarrassment in the gallery.

Parties in the Careys were always an entertainment, intentional or otherwise. I have already mentioned their similarity to the Percy French parties, but whereas those earlier parties had usually ended musically (or, at least, more or less so) the parties I enjoyed always ended in charades after supper. One feature of the evening was always the Poetry Game in which a given subject and a question had to be answered, or at least encompassed in a minimum of four lines of verse. Frequently screeds of what seemed at the time brilliant verse were produced, but perhaps it is as well that the end of the evening the whole lot went into the fire for it might not have appeared so amusing in the cold light of morning. If Clerihews had not already been invented, Arthur McCabe would have done so, for with his usual contempt for convention he fitted the most outrageous rhymes into equally irregular rhythms, and his efforts were always greeted with howls of mixed horror and delight. Another guest without whom no Carey party was complete was a friend called Nelson. He would give the most hilarious one-man sketches, impersonating all manner of people. His performances were always impromptu, nothing written down, nothing rehearsed, feeding on his audience's appreciation, and so nothing remains of them either but the grateful memory.

Sometimes parties would simply develop by themselves without invitations and when that happened Mary would fetch a bowl from the kitchen and begin beating the ingredients for her buns, which were her speciality. She would sit on the floor by the hearth, warming the bowl in her lap and talking to her guests. Then the buns would be popped in the oven and forgotten, until someone would say, 'Mary, I think I can smell your buns,' and we would all have tea.

Once when preparing for an invited party she went to light the oven with the last match, which promptly blew out. She then went through the house looking for another box, after which there followed quite an explosion.

'Yes,' said Mary as, eyebrowless, she welcomed her guests, 'I feel a bomb could do nothing to me now.'

Looking back it is hard to say what brought all the Careys' friends together. We never formed any artistic circle or anything like that. We simply enjoyed the Careys and, possibly because we had all been reared in more conventional households, we relished their unusual way of looking at life. What worried other people never bothered them. Little mishaps which others might have quietly buried were laughingly related, and even what might have been hurtful moments were laughed off too. As when Mary, passing through an auctioneer's room one day saw a painting of her father's and said to her friend: 'I wonder how much that will fetch?' One of the porters turned round and said: 'Well now, mind you, there's some as'll buy that kinda thing.'

One of the most constant of the Careys' 'regulars' was Freddie, a vehement arguer and first class bridge player, although bridge was never played at the Careys. Unfortunately he was plagued with asthma all his life and died in his early forties. His brother Philip figured frequently at Carey gatherings before he went to live in England. His hobby was heraldry and he was only too delighted to prove to you that some eminent personage or institution had no right to display certain heraldic devices. For a time he studied music in London, hoping to become a conductor, and related how he had turned over two pages of the score together and how, when, as he thought, he had brought the orchestra to a triumphant finale, they cantered on for another two pages without him. Sensing perhaps that a conductorship was not for him, he applied for the post of Blue Mantel Pursuivant, which would have entitled him to wear a most magnificent costume on State occasions.

'Well Philip,' said Mrs. Carey, 'if you get this post, you must promise to visit me in your full regalia — on one condition — that you come in a cab with drawn blinds.'

However he did not get the post, but made contact with a number of people with kindred interests and eventually took himself off to Canterbury, where for many years he ran an office dealing with heraldic claims and entitlements.

Another visitor, Kay, had one of her paintings accepted by the Royal Academy but has since remained all her life a happy amateur, painting only for her own and her friends' pleasure.

In fact all the Carey's friends did their own thing in their own way simply for the fun of it and none of them made commercial use of their gifts. Even Mr. Carey put a low price on his pictures, which was sometimes overruled by Mrs. Carey who was more in touch with the housekeeping bills.

Then one day Nelson interrupted this dilletante atmosphere by announcing that he had got a job in the talks department of the B.B.C. We marvelled to think of one of our number set up in an office with secretaries at his beck and call. However, Nelson never seemed very happy in it, and when he finally left the job, Mrs. Carey said: 'Nelson is like a bird that has got its wings back.'

Nelson eventually became head of the English Department in the Technical College and wrote a book on the Irish writer Le Fanu. He and Bartley, who for some reason was always known by his surname, were the only two of the circle who could be said to have disginguished themselves academically. Bartley became Professor of English first in an Indian university and later in Wales, but although he was an intimate friend of the family, by the time I was enjoying the Careys' parties he was already in India and made his contribution to the evening through the letters he wrote from there. Alan in America contributed too, as when in answer to a questionnaire sent by his anxious mother enquiring about his health and what he took for lunch, he replied; 'Monica, but she pays her own.'

Another occasional guest was Tommy. I say occasional, because he would disappear from time to time on board one of the Finnish windjammers, which up to the beginning of the Second World War still sailed between Belfast and Australia. An exotic postcard would arrive and then nothing more would be heard from Tommy, until coming down to breakfast some morning they would find him asleep on the sofa.

One evening when Tommy had returned from some of his voyages and was regaling us with accounts of life before the mast Freddie arrived to say that there was a wasps' nest in the lane behind their house. At once everyone made suggestions. Mary ran upstairs and came back with an ancient wide-brimmed straw hat and a net curtain. As Tommy was the tallest — well over six feet — and had probably the longest reach, the hat was placed on his head and Mary tacked the curtain round the brim. Then he was driven in a small Austin 7 to the scene of action, accompanied by as many as could squeeze into such a modest vehicle.

All appeared to be going well until a wasp found the way inside the curtain, whereupon Tommy sought asylum in the car, but the others, seeing the swarm of angry wasps that were following

Tommy, reversed at speed all the way down Knockdene Park, pursued by this wildly gesticulating ghost in the straw hat, in its turn pursued by the wasps.

It was small wonder that Angela, the cat, found it so fascinating to sit in her gazebo, observing the antics of the neighbourhood.

13

In many ways Molly Greeves, another friend, should be writing this book, not I. She and the three Carey children had shared a governess before they were sent to school, and her house is full of relics of the Careys which she has kindly allowed me to see and enjoy. She has an illuminated address presented to her aunt, who for many years was organist at the British and Foreign Sailors' Society's Church, and which Mr. Carey has surrounded with the most charming little seascapes framed in lifebelts. This was the delicate miniature type of work at which he excelled, and I feel sure there must be many more examples of it in hidden corners of the Province.

The Greeves and the Carey parents were old friends and neighbours and frequently spent Sunday evenings together in the Greeves' house, but because it was the Sabbath, Mrs. Carey insisted that the subjects chosen for the drawing-guessing game should all be taken from the Bible. I have already described how at the end of an evening in the Careys' everything went into the fire, but at the Greeves's evenings Mr. Greeves so prized Mr. Carey's illustrations, which were done in pencil on any old bits of paper, that he kept them, and they are still a delight.

By 1928 both pairs of parents decided that as they had never done very much about the further education of their daughters they would send them to live with a French family outside Paris for three months. They arrived in January of what was an exceptionally cold winter when there were chunks of ice floating on the Seine and the large tiled stove which heated their room never seemed to get the heat down to their feet. Molly suffered extremely from chilblains.

The possibility of taking a bath raised enormous problems. Madame discouraged the idea as being injurious to health and only to be undertaken if one remained in bed all day afterwards. The bath itself was like some sort of cauldron, being heated by gas from below, which surely must have made the metal too hot to sit on...? But perhaps these are questions best left unanswered, and I only mention the matter because it seems astonishing that both the bath and Madame's views on bathing existed in 1928.

Mary, who had left school ten years previously, learnt to speak French tolerably well — she may have inherited some of old Aunt Catharine Pasche's flair for languages — but her behaviour puzzled the French household. At home Mary never ate a proper meal at the table at the same time as everyone else, but existed on eating odd bits of things at odd times. She became a very good cook and would be delighted to put some delicious dish on the table, but then would retire without tasting it and was happiest when allowed to curl up on her bed for the afternoon with a book. Madame suspected that she was ill, possibly pregnant?... and that Molly was trying to help and protect her friend.

When they went home they bought presents for their families, and Mary expedited their passage through the Customs by buying a ripe Camembert cheese for her father. When the Customs Officer opened her case he closed it again at once.

14

There is something about the words 'English visitor' which at once causes men in these parts to straighten their ties and women to flick the crumbs from their skirts. Such was the effect on the Careys when my brother Morris announced that he was going to marry not only an English girl, but the daughter of a colonel in the regular army. 'You must bring her over some evening,' said Mrs. Carey primly. 'I'll let you know which evening would suit Mr. Carey.' This seemed to me an astonishingly stiff invitation to a house where invitations had never before been necessary and where people had simply dropped in at all hours of the day and night.

When the appointed evening arrived and we entered the drawing room I noticed that the unstable pile of music and papers, which usually stood at one end of the piano, now stood at the other end. Some of the ornaments had changed places too, none of which greatly altered the appearance of the room, but suggested that possibly a duster had passed that way. The chairs, too, had a new look. I have already described one of Mrs. Carey's methods of freshening the faded parts of cretonne. Another method was to spread odd remnants of cretonne loosely over the chairs, so that when you sat down they folded themselves endearingly around you, and when you got up you found they had formed a clinging attachment. But to-night all was neatness. I sat down gingerly, suspecting glue, and was relieved to discover tacking threads. Of Angela and her brood not a trace was to be seen, although it was not by sight alone that you sensed there were cats in the house.

At parties when he was not busy with his pencil, Mr. Carey would sit stiffly upright, tightly buttoned in his best suit, his knees demurely pressed together and his idle hands folded on his lap, as if he were waiting for some family funeral service to begin. Once when squashed tightly on a sofa between Mrs. Carey and another lady who were both carrying on animated conversations with their neighbours on either hand, Mrs. Carey turned to him and said: 'Now Joe, isn't it time you said something?' only to find that, wedged bolt upright, he had nodded over. I hoped he was not going to nod over now.

Mrs. Carey, however, kept the conversation going, which was also strange in this house where conversation had always burbled along, sometimes shooting off into side issues and sometimes boiling over, but never needing to be helped along by its hostess.

We chatted rather stiffly about this and that and I realized regretfully that such was the influence of my English sister-in-law-to-be that the Careys were really not being themselves at all. They were very nearly being ordinary.

Presently Bruce was despatched to put the kettle on. After some time Mary disappeared to see what was keeping the tea. Still no tea arrived, and in the lulls in the conversation, now becoming more frequent, we were aware of whispering and peculiar shufflings and bumpings outside the door. Finally I was sent to investigate.

At first sight Mary and Bruce appeared to be playing bears in the almost total darkness of the passage leading to the kitchen.

'Well, I was told to shut up all the cats in the kitchen,' explained Bruce.

'But you weren't told to lock them in, idiot,' hissed Mary, 'nor to lose the key.'

'There's a hole in that pocket,' said Bruce.

'The kettle isn't on, then?' I ventured, wondering if I should offer to run home and boil one there.

'Oh yes, I climbed in over the yard wall,' said Bruce.

'And it is about time you climbed back again and turned it off,' said Mary. 'I wonder the steam isn't coming through the key-hole by now.'

'If you two came round to the pantry window,' suggested Bruce, 'I could pass you out the tea tray and we could bring it round to the front door,' but fortunately, before that could be put into action, one of us knelt on the key.

No number of English visitors could ever prevent the Careys from being themselves.

15

The Careys always had tremendous enthusiasm for starting things, like redecorating a room or digging up some part of the garden, but few of these projects, even if finished, ever turned out as first envisaged. I have already mentioned the breeding of pure Persian cats and the hand-painted crockery. To these should be added Mrs. Carey's decision to paint the surrounds of her bedroom floor, which she did most successfully, only to find that she had left herself marooned in the middle. She had been working in fluffy bedroom slippers and, not wanting to get them sticky, she took them off. The same applied to her stockings, so in the end she walked out in her bare feet, which explains why in the spring, when the landing carpets were lifted, Man Friday's foot prints could be seen heading for the bathroom.

The writer Joyce Cary spells his name differently, yet I feel he bears a strong family resemblance, more especially through the characters in his books. His potted biography in the paperback editions states that 'he came of a Devonshire family long settled in Ireland', which also describes the Careys, who were pleased that Kingsley in *Westward Ho* had chosen the name Will Carey for one of his characters. It may be pure coincidence, but certainly, when I read the description of Olly Jimson's mural masterpiece in *The Horse's Mouth*, I could not help remembering the pattern of Mrs. Carey's feet.

The project, most deplored by the users of the shortcut, was its conversion to a crazy pavement. 'A right name for it,' as one of them said sourly. The operation took a very long time, involved a lot of digging, quantities of flagstones, a great many forgotten tools and implements, and a vagueness about the precise edges of the path, which made it quite unsafe to use after dark. It would have been the perfect deterrent to the message boys, as indeed it became to many others. As was customary with the Careys' undertakings, everyone stopped to offer comment or advice. Arthur McCabe, I noticed, seemed to take great interest in the path's progress, even to the extent of helping to lay the stones, which was most unlike Arthur. Mary rewarded his labours with innumerable cups of tea. It was when the path had just passed the front door that they announced their engagement, after which, I need not say, the path never progressed another inch. For years afterwards shortcutters, stumbling over that abrupt end of craziness, were to bless the spot where Mary had said yes.

The engagement took nearly everyone by surprise for Mary had never seemed to be the sort of person who got married. She was the first to admit this herself. Nor was Arthur really the marrying type either, but as Mrs. Greeves said: 'How well suited they are because they are both a bit odd, and that would save upsetting two households.'

As the preparations for the wedding progressed the pile of sewing to be done grew, until it seemed that it would never be finished in time. 'Here,' said Mrs. Dickson, who had dropped in, 'give me a needle and I'll finish that.'

'Mother dear,' said Mary, 'where is our needle?'

A large party was held before the wedding at which I remember seeing Mr. Carey, who was not well acquainted with such things, holding a tumbler to the handle of a siphon of lemonade — there was never anything stronger at Carey parties — and hopefully pressing the nozzle. It was not the usual sort of Carey party because there were far too many people, in fact the house seemed to bulge with them, and in the midst of all the commotion I heard Mrs. Carey deploring to someone that Arthur had not yet arrived. Mary, passing with a plate of cakes, said: 'Who hasn't come, mother dear?'

For all that they were married the next day quietly and without fuss and went to live in a small bungalow at Dundonald where Mary tried hard, until the novelty wore off, to be an ordinary housewife.

However, Mary was not long in her little bungalow before her father died in 1937 at the age of eighty-seven, to be followed a year later by Mrs. Carey. No-one knew her age — she always claimed to be 'forty on my last birthday'.

So Mary, with Arthur, returned to the house across the way to keep house for Bruce, and although I was delighted to have her back I missed her parents sadly.

'The Gobbins' by J. W. Carey.

Part Two

Mary and Arthur

16

Mrs. Carey had always taken a great interest in the cases which came before her as a J.P. and tried to help them to make a new start. She and Mary encouraged one young man to marry his girl friend and to settle down and make a home for themselves. This advice may have been well meant, but it was unrealistic. If he had had difficulties before, to saddle the young man with a wife and family was like hanging a millstone round his neck and it was not long before he was in trouble again. Feeling responsible for the advice she and her mother had given, Mary persuaded Arthur that they should adopt one of the children.

And so one day I was surprised to meet Mary walking down the Park with a small brown-eyed child of about three.

'This is Emily,' said Mary, 'we are going to adopt her.'

So Emily joined the family, to be followed soon after by Shandy, a large liver and white woolly dog, a near relation of a retriever maybe, whose little red-rimmed pheasant's eyes were far too small for his large, foolish face.

Mary became a devoted mother and dog owner, although she was soon heard to remark that she wished someone would invent dog's paw patterned linoleum.

When the Second World War broke out Mary, like everyone else, did her best about the black-out, but was rather less successful than the rest of us. In her case there were peculiar difficulties. Nearly all the windows downstairs jutted out in bays all round the house which, as Mary said, would have taken miles of black-out material, so she attempted to seal off the bays from the rest of the room by one straight curtain. As this reduced the size of the rooms, people were always brushing against the curtains and disarranging them so that shafts of light escaped, not, as Mary said, that they could have been seen from the air because of the overhanging roof of the bay window. Arthur quickly realized that if the war were to be pursued in any degree of peace and amicability he must at once become the

Air Raid Warden for the Park, which he did. Thereafter the neighbourhood spent the rest of the war in tranquillity, immune to the acrimonious arguments about chinks and moth-holes.

Arthur ran his own business in a small shop in Queen Street, styled 'Radio Development', although, as it was staffed by himself, an assistant and an office boy, the 'development' could only have been limited. Nevertheless, he secured contracts from the Ministry of Defence by which he had to drive round in his van, making announcements through the loudspeaker. Mary went with him. She said it was astonishing how the people ran out of their houses and, because it was Arthur's voice coming over the speaker, they expected him to be able to answer all their queries. One man wanted to know if he was to send his pigeons to the Reception Centre, and another explained that he could not be evacuated because his sow was due to farrow.

'I had no idea there was so much livestock in Ballymacarett,' said Mary.

My brother Morris had joined the Territorials in 1938 and was commissioned at the outbreak of war. The 8th Anti-Aircraft Regiment was recruited very largely from the Shankill Road, but in those days the significance of 'the Shankill' and 'the Falls' was probably lost on the billetting officer for when they arrived in France they found themselves billetted, of all places, in an evacuated convent. Morris said he never thought to see the Virgin girt around with Orange sashes. Daily, distraught and voluble French nuns came running with tales of woe, and after one large portrait of the Pope which stood at the head of the stairs had met with an accident, Morris found himself conducting a post-mortem over its ashes.

'No, no sir,' said one fervent Orangeman, 'it wasn't me that burned him — I only carried him down.'

Over which we will draw a veil.

Winston McCabe, Arthur's brother, joined up at the beginning of the war and served in the ranks until he was commissioned. At the same time his great friend, who was a Roman Catholic, joined with him and on their first Sunday in camp in Cornwall, when the various denominations were called to step forward and be marched off to their different churches, Win feared that his friend might be the only Roman Catholic. So he, who had been reared amongst the

Plymouth Brethren, stepped forward with him.

A gasp rippled through the ranks: 'A couple of bloody Papishes!'

I have no doubt that Win's sudden conversion was brought about out of consideration for his friend. Nevertheless it had not escaped their notice that, whereas other denominations were faced with a short sharp march to their places of worship, the Roman Catholic chapel was so far away it could only be reached with an army vehicle and, after allowing for mistakes in map-reading, it could easily have taken them all day to get back to camp.

For the Mess Concert Morris wrote and, what is more, sang the following paraphrase of the Mountains of Mourne, perhaps an echo of a Carey party performance.

Oh Mary this .... is a wonderful town,
It's bigger than any in ould County Down,
You should see the shops with their windows all lit,
There's no air raid wardens to issue a writ.
It's no wonder them Nazis haven't dared to appear,
I think they must know that the 8th are all here
But for all that I've shot at I might as well be
Where the Mountains of Mourne sweep down to the sea.

The Frenchies are decent, but don't speak our way,
It's the hell of a job making out what they say.
We try to be pleasant so as not to be rude
But we felt more at home when we stayed down in Bude.
When pay day comes round we are paid all in francs,
With the notes that we get, you would think we owned banks,
Still give me a bob and I'd much rather be,
Where the Mountains of Mourne sweep down to the sea.

Well Mary, the weather has been pretty tough
But we've jerkins and scarves and helmets enough.
I've so many clothes that I'm sure that my pack
Won't hold the half of them slung on my back.
The food's not too bad though strange to be told
The spuds are that scarce, you would think they were gold,
So you won't find it hard to satisfy me
Where the Mountains of Mourne sweep down to the sea.

Now don't you be sending me cigarettes here
As they cost next to nothing and so does the beer,
In fact it's that aisy to come by good drink,
It's the devil's own job keeping out of the clink.
Still I'll be ready, when leave comes along,
To pack up for home with a smile and a song
To the wild rose I know well that's waiting for me
Where the Mountains of Mourne sweep down to the sea.

On his first leave home Win decided to treat Mary and Emily to lunch in town on his last day. He indulged Emily in too many ice-creams and then their programme got behind because the poor child wanted to spend a penny so frequently. When I dropped over to say goodbye to Win I found Mary running round distractedly.

'These things are not nearly dry enough to pack and I have still got socks to darn, and the train goes at five.'

'Give me the iron,' I said, 'and I'll try and dry them.'

Win appeared and stood grinning in the doorway.

'You know,' he said, 'some day when Morris is proudly marching at the head of his men I'm going to get a great kick out of telling the chaps beside me — back home his sister irons my shirts.'

Sometime between the invasion of the Netherlands and the fall of France, when we were not very sure where our army was, I dropped in on my way back from shopping.

Mary was curled up on the sofa, reading the paper spread beside her, whilst eating spoonfuls of jam. In all the years I knew Mary I cannot ever remember seeing her eating a proper meal at a proper table.

'The news is bad,' I said.

'Isn't it?' said Mary, 'and nobody seems to be able to do anything. Just look at what Lord Halifax has been saying,' indicating long columns in the paper, 'and you know how slowly they speak in parliament. Though who am I to talk about doing things, sitting here eating jam that I ought to be saving up.'

Emily and Shandy, the dog, were sharing a lollipop by a process of alternate licks, and at this moment she noticed them. The lollipop was banished to the mantelpiece from where it somersaulted into the exposed innards of a wireless set Arthur had been mending and remained inextricably fixed. I wondered if sticky sugar transmitted or insulated electricity and how Arthur would explain its presence to his customer.

When Emily had stopped crying, Mary said: 'Do you know where Morris is?'

'Not exactly. He fixed a code with Nancy on condition she wouldn't tell, so all we know is that he is in a relatively safe place.'

'Oh yes, I did that with Win. But then I lost my end of it, and now I can't make top nor tail of his letters. They're all so full of the most peculiar statements — it would be so interesting if only I knew what he meant. The Income Tax people wrote to him yesterday, but I just sent it back to them with a note saying "is somewhere between France and Belgium, but I should not worry him about this just now, as I expect he has other things to think about".'

Later that summer, when invasion seemed imminent, I and other 'droppers-in' began asking each other what each of us would do, should a German paratrooper appear in the doorway. 'I should look him straight in the eye,' said Mary, 'and say: "Was würde Ihre Mutter sagen?"'

It could have been an interesting encounter.

When the bombs eventually fell on Belfast in the following spring Mary would shuffle out through the flickering darkness and the scattering shrapnel to bring glasses of warm milk to nervous old ladies. And then Shandy would get out after her and bark furiously, and then we would hear Arthur's voice trying to get both of them in again, so that it was not by reason of the bombs only that no one got much sleep. Long after the All Clear the Careys' gate still wheezed and clanged, and the door knocker stuttered. As the raids continued Arthur suggested that it would be better if all the old ladies came to his house for their warm milk, but later Mary said that he completely destroyed the reassuring atmosphere she had tried so hard to create, by remarking, as he surveyed the assortment of feet radiating out from under the dining room table, 'If this house is hit the casualties are going to be phenomenal.'

Bruce had joined the RNVR and by chance had been stationed in Belfast, engaged in minesweeping; in fact one of his jobs after the air raids was to search for mines in the Belfast Water Works. One evening he and some of his brother officers, groping their way in the blackout from pub to pub, met Stewart, another resident of Knockdene Park, and a game of poker was suggested as a pleasanter entertainment. Stewart said he would join them later and they made their way to the house at Knock.

The poker game started, but one of their number became very tiresome, arguing and spoiling the game, so that eventually they threw him out and locked the door. He knocked and clamoured to be let in, but in the end went off and fell asleep in one of the cars.

The game then proceeded in peace until there was a fresh burst of knocking at the door. Quite forgetting that they had invited Stewart, they shouted abuse at the knocker and suggested, not very politely, where he might go. Stewart, who was a big man and who had recently been promoted to the rank of major, swelled with indignation and redoubled his hammering with the door knocker. Suddenly the door opened and he was flung down the steps, after which, as they say, there was the mother and father of a row.

Bruce next day in his letter of apology and explanation said he was very sorry he had hit Stewart when the others were holding him, 'but it seemed such a good opportunity', a statement which did little to heal the breach. In fact, a coolness was perpetuated afterwards by Win and Stewart cutting each other dead every time they met in Alexandria.

Mary said she was so glad that whilst all this was going on downstairs her Arthur was safely tucked up in bed beside her. I wonder myself what Mrs. Carey might have had to say about that night's affray.

17

In the summer of 1940 Arthur bought a boat, a fact which is to pervade the rest of this chronicle and alter its focus. It was an open centreboard boat, eighteen feet long, with a silly little jib and an enormous gaff-rigged mainsail. It was painted red and named *Margaret*, and because I had begun sailing a small racing dinghy a few years earlier, Arthur looked to me to advise him in all things nautical. Knowing his performances in cars and on motor-bicycles, I had mixed feelings about going sailing with him, and I was even more doubtful about *Margaret's* behaviour. It was alleged that she did not capsize, but I had no means of knowing how far she had been provoked in this direction or to what lengths Arthur might go. However, when he asked me to come with them one baking hot

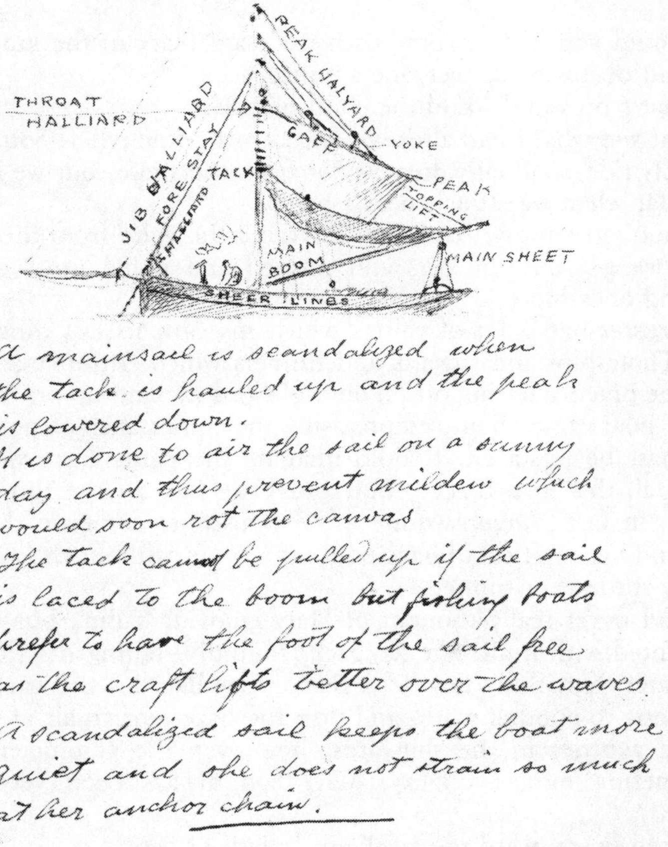

'Parts of a boat' from J. W. Carey's sketchbook.

afternoon, I agreed readily enough because there was absolutely no wind, and I felt that if Arthur's motive power were curtailed at source his exuberance might be kept within reason.

Margaret was moored among the mudflats at Whitehouse where Arthur had bought her. A small boy on the end of the jetty languidly watched us as Mary, Emily, Arthur and myself clambered in.

'Would you like to come with us?' said Mary in the kindly way she had of involving everyone around.

'Thar's no wund,' said the child bluntly.

That was what I had already noticed with some relief. Something, possibly tide, gradually drew us out from the shore, but we had not gone far when we crunched to a halt.

'Thon's the musselbank yer on,' came the voice from the jetty.

So we got out the oars and pushed and poled until we were drifting once more.

Margaret had a lot of things which my Snipe Class dinghy had not. Thole-pins and thwarts and runners which Arthur made Mary and me practice letting off on one side and making up on the other as the boat came about, emphasising the importance of not letting the mast be unstayed. I could imagine the panic there would be doing all this in a breeze, but to-day we had all the time in the world, in fact *Margaret* quite often refused to come on the other tack and her mast could have borne the strain without the assistance of any shrouds or runners.

I had never really thought of Mary enjoying sailing but she was enchanted with it all. She sat back languidly trailing her fingers in the water, remarking how on a perfect day like this the war seemed to belong to another world and how the haze lent an air of mystery to the gantries in the shipyards, how even the gasometer had a shimmering mirage quality. Mary had always been very short-sighted.

Presently we heard the creak and splash of oars.

'I'm going after driftwood. Will I give yez a tow?' at which Arthur said something.

'He was only trying to be helpful, dear,' said Mary.

Arthur stored the boat that winter in Carnalea and next spring asked me if I would help sail it in stages to Strangford Lough. He knew someone with enough petrol to drive us to Carnalea and we should come back by train from Donaghadee. Although I still had misgivings about Arthur's sailing and the boat's performance and, above all, about the bar at the entrance to Strangford, I thought nothing very much could happen to us on the first leg. I even suggested that my young cousin, who lived in Groomsport and was showing an interest in sailing, might come too, and her mother invited us to stop there for lunch.

When we arrived at the boatyard in Carnalea a fresh easterly wind was crashing a nasty sea straight on to the slipway, making most unfavourable conditions for launching. However, the men of the yard declared it could be done and they would tow us out to a mooring so that we could hoist sail. The mast had been stepped, but all the other gear, sails, spars and ropes were simply dumped in a heap in the bottom of the boat. We were told to get in and then were given a tremendous shove. We trundled off down the slipway, as in a tumbril to the guillotine, hit the water with a splash, managed to catch the tow rope, reach the mooring and eventually get the sails up, but by the time we had done that young Cherrie had turned green.

Apart from this, the beat across Bangor Bay was very pleasant. The sea sparkled in the sun and the wind, although fresh, was steady. As we neared Groomsport I suggested to Arthur that it might be better to come in at the north end of Cockle island, but he would not agree. I pointed out that with the wind behind us we should come through the harbour entrance very fast, that the tide was already more than half out, that there seemed to be a good many boats in the harbour, that we could see better what water there was if we came in the other way, but he was deaf to all suggestions, and eventually I fell silent. I felt that Arthur was simply using my presence on board with my supposed knowledge of sailing as a reassurance to Mary and an excuse for him to do daft things.

White water was breaking at the eastern end of Cockle and where it met the backwash from the harbour wall it threw up jagged spikes of water. In that confused sea, if *Margaret* ran too dead, she could accidentally gybe and possibly roll right over.

I suppose had I been a man I should simply have pushed Arthur aside and taken the tiller from him, but being a woman I began to make contingency plans. I wondered what effect sudden immersion had on the seasick. By the look of Cherrie, it seemed drowning would be most welcome. I was not worried about Arthur. With his long legs he would soon touch bottom anyway.

Suddenly Arthur interrupted my thoughts.

'You know this place better than I do. I think you'd better take her in.'

There were a lot of things I would like to have said to Arthur, but there was no time just then.

Meantime, on shore, my aunt had just concluded a deal with John, the vegetable man.

'And where is Miss Cherrie the day?' he asked.

'She has gone sailing with some friends,' said my aunt, 'I think this might be them coming in now.'

'Mrs. Lytle dear, you should never have let Miss Cherrie out with them ones. Them ones is daft.'

Had I heard him I could not have agreed with him more.

At first I had a wild idea of throwing up head to wind and getting down that enormous mainsail, but then I was not sure if *Margaret's* tiny jib would maintain steerage way. The anchor was somewhere underneath all the pile of gear under Cherrie's lifeless form and, in any case, the rocks of Cockle were already far too close for comfort.

I decided instead to cut as close as I dared to the point of Cockle and aim slantwise for the end of the harbour, and thus avoid running dead. As we turned away from the wind our speed increased and then a big wave lifted the stern so that the rudder had little influence on our direction. At the same moment I saw that on the end of the harbour was a horrid iron ladder to which *Margaret's* stumpy little bowsprit seemed to be drawn as to a magnet. Just when impact seemed unavoidable the wave on which we were riding began to peel off along the harbour wall and, slapping broadside into *Margaret*, dumped her inside the harbour. If ever a boat was asked to perform a stop-Kristiania, *Margaret* was then.

When I opened my eyes again, a number of fishermen had opened theirs very wide indeed, so I at once stood up and tried to pretend that everything had gone according to plan and that I had never for one moment doubted it might be otherwise.

Then I saw that, although there were a great many boats, there was just space enough for us between them and found to my joy that we had just enough way left to glide into it. To have come roaring into a small harbour under full sail, rounded up and yet reserved enough momentum to be able to glide into a berth which, until we came round the corner I had not known existed, now this was really something that people would tell their children and their children's children...

But Arthur, to whom the need to stop had also become apparent, shattered my dreams by letting all halliards fly at once. The boom, followed almost instantly by the gaff, plummetted between me and Cherrie, killing neither of us. Arthur who had been standing before the mast, unfortunately was not killed either.

18

Although the wind dropped after lunch, Cherrie did not venture farther, and Arthur and I continued towards Donaghadee without her.

For the first ten years of my life my parents had rented houses in Ballywilliam for the summer months, and as the coast slipped slowly by, I remembered holidays I had spent there, the little bays where we had paddled and learnt to swim, the rocks we had learnt to dive off. When landing was again permitted after the First World War I remembered going on a picnic to the larger Copeland Island which was still inhabited by various branches of a family called Clegg, and how in one of the cottages we found the women churning by hand. I was astonished to be told that butter could be made by thumping up and down in that revolting smelly old barrel, and I went out into the fresh air, whilst the grown-ups enthused over the whole process with the women.

I was a puny child with an easily upset stomach and a sensitive and impressionable nose. I remember marvelling how some distant cousins could possibly spend the summer in a house called Glenburnie because of the pervading smell of the nearby scutch mill. I suppose there are children growing up in Ulster today who have never smelt retted flax. I can assure them it is pungent, similar to that of the pig-sty, but for me and, I am sure for many a faraway exile it will always bring back a whiff of home.

At this point perhaps I might explain why it is that I am known to some as Betty and others as Honor, because I think it was during that summer that I first decided to take the matter into my own hands. I had been christened Honor Elizabeth and my mother dithered. In fact, I had been christened Alice Honor Elizabeth, Alice for my mother's older sister but she never intended me to be called Alice, on that point she did not dither, but was subsequently persuaded, probably by the same sister, that Honor was far too stiff and grown-up for a baby. So I began as Betty.

That summer, the last summer of the Kaiser's war, when we stayed in Ballywilliam and the cousins at Portavo the distance between us presented no difficulties because everyone had bicycles — all except me that is. I was delighted when suddenly they swept into the garden and began some game. If it was cricket I never got much of a share of the batting, usually being sent to field far away near the hedge where I became inattentive and absorbed in popping the globes of fuchsia. Then suddenly some new idea would sieze them and they would vanish like a flock of starlings. It could have been a most provoking summer for me had not Colin, the oldest of the cousins, been big enough in stature and kindliness to take me on his handle-bars. I loved Colin dearly, except for one thing. He would call me Lizzie, and what should have been an irresistible invitation, 'Come on Lizzie, I'll take you,' was very hard to accept. I therefore decided that when I went to school I should simply say I was called Honor, which I did, but because I was a puny child I was kept at home with a governess until I was nine, so the Bettys had a good start.

Colin's house was permitted a key for the door in the garden wall which led into Portavo demesne, and once when we had all gone into the woods to look for blackberries an airship loomed monstrously above the tree-tops. Colin, I remember, was most reassuring, checking my impulse to head for home as fast as I could, and explaining that it was one of ours which had come over from Whitehead.

Later, when I could ride a bicycle and was sent to do the messages in Donaghadee, my nose enjoyed the smell of freshly baked baps which I fetched from the baker. As a perk I was allowed to spend twopence of the change on an ice-cream slider, and no ice-cream ever since has tasted quite so delicious. I remember too the warm earthy smell of Mrs. Jamison's greenhouse and the peaches which her gardener plucked and placed almost reverently in my basket.

Mrs. Jamison was a remarkable old lady. She had never lost her youthful enthusiasm for bathing and in particular a passion, acquired in later life, for sliding down the chute. She lived opposite the swimming pool and, realizing that her costume was rather out-of-date and her figure not suited to a modern one, she would slip across the road before breakfast and indulge her pleasure before anyone was about. The attendant always put a bucket of water down the chute before she came, but one morning he was late and Mrs. Jamison began her descent on a bone-dry slide. Fearing that the seat of her antique costume might not be equal to the friction, she gripped the sides of the chute and remained there, perched like the fairy on the Christmas tree, until the apologetic and near apoplectic attendant sluiced her on her way.

That long forgotten airship, I suppose, was patrolling the creeks and inlets of Co. Down on the lookout for lurking submarines, although I cannot think that the German Naval Intelligence, being certainly better informed about the peculiarities of Donaghadee Sound than either Arthur or I were at this period of our sailing experience, would ever have hazarded one of their U-boats anywhere near the place.

Donaghadee Sound is a curious place where the tide flows for nine hours in one direction and three in the other, and by the time it is nearing the end of its nine hours' flow it has built up a great mass of water, trying to get back. A place, in fact, where no knowledgeable yachtsman, or indeed anyone in their right mind goes near if they can possibly avoid it. Arthur and I, however, were quite unaware of such things as we sailed blissfully towards them. Suddenly we found ourselves skimming over a mirror-smooth lake of water towards a towering wall of breakers and a few moments later, in a smother of spray, we hit it with such force that the goose-neck of the boom jumped clean off the mast and the boom stuck out in front. As I struggled to get it on again before it could tear the sail I glanced back at Arthur with some irritation. There were trickles creeping down my neck and I was beginning to feel that the events of the day were becoming less entertaining. But Arthur was sitting there with an enchanted grin on his face, drops of water glistening on his spectacles and a jewel-bright drip on the lobe of each impish ear.

'You should never have come through there,' said a nautical type, as we landed at Donaghadee. We agreed, but as I have said earlier of his motoring, there was some guardian angel presiding over Arthur who allowed him to do these things and get away with them.

Years later, when Arthur had progressed to bigger and better boats and had sailed round Ireland, someone, marvelling at this performance, said to me: 'But would you really consider him an experienced yachtsman?'

'Very,' I said. But I doubt if I meant it as he did.

19

Mary and Arthur had rented the two-storeyed farmhouse on Eileenmore in Ringhaddy Sound, and soon *Margaret* was safely moored in the little bay opposite the house. This house, like the one at Knock, became a place which people casually dropped into, only here they came by boat and frequently stayed the night. Somehow Mary coped with the unknown number of visitors who might or might not remember to bring their rations with them, and I enjoyed many weekends on the island.

Freddie felt the fresh air did his asthma good and was a frequent visitor. Bruce spent all his leaves there, and Cherrie, undeterred by her previous experience, came down too. She and Arthur discovered most of the pladdies and reefs in Strangford Lough by getting stuck on them, and when that happened Arthur lifted Margaret's centreboard and they simply pushed, bumped, and rocked themselves over the obstruction. In this way *Margaret* made passages that no boat has ever done before or since, yet she never seemed to suffer any damage. Arthur was completely bitten by the sailing bug, but at this stage none of us could persuade him to learn to tie proper knots. He was always too impulsive, too impatient, always wanting to be off, and when he tied things together they soon pulled into tangles that were impossible to undo.

Once I arrived in a borrowed boat of the Viking Class, a bit bigger than my own, and found Arthur, Mary, Emily and Freddie sailing about in *Margaret* with another friend, Glen, paddling after them in his canoe. Arthur at once was interested in the Viking and wanted to see how it sailed then and there, although it was already quite late in the evening. He asked Glen to take the family home and leave the canoe tied behind *Margaret*, so that we could pick it up and paddle ourselves ashore.

We had quite a pleasant little sail and, after picking up the canoe in the gathering dusk, we withdrew to a safe distance from *Margaret* and dropped anchor. Of course we dropped it in that part of the bay where the tide is strong and the bottom stoney and so, instead of holding fast in soft sinking mud, it gently trailed itself along the bottom. But Arthur and I were far too busy taking down the sails to notice and it was only when we went to get into the canoe that we found it was nearly on the shore, and worse, that there was a nasty barbed-wire fence, intended to keep cattle from straying at low tide which ran far out into the water, close to the Viking. There was not much hope of pulling the Viking clear with the canoe, so we bellowed for the others to bring down the dinghy. Eventually after what seemed ages Mary and Freddie appeared, Glen having gone after mushrooms, and eventually they got the dinghy launched. Arthur jumped into it to help Freddie row and I threw him the end of the anchor rope. Freddie then had an attack of his asthma and Arthur caught a crab which landed him on his back, but I was reassured to see, out of the corner of my eye, Mary perched precariously on the fence armed with a floor-mop with which to fend us off. Sometimes just at sundown a little breeze springs up which is what happened then, and hoping to help the rowers who were not making much progress, I pulled up the jib. At which the Viking began to tow the dinghy backwards by the stern, so that it was in danger of going under.

'Let us go,' shouted Arthur.

'You let your end go,' I cried, 'I can sail her off.'

But his end was tied with one of his impossible knots and mine, which had the anchor on its outer end, had been clovehitched round the mast, so there was nothing to be done but drop the jib again.

Happily another dinghy happened to pass by and they towed us clear and showed us where we ought to have dropped the anchor, and so Mary did not need to use the floor-mop after all.

Mary was happy on the island and did not mind in the least being left there, whilst Arthur went off on some new exploration. They hung a swing for Emily from the apple tree, and Mary was often to be found lying back in a deck chair in the shade of the tree, reading or reciting to Emily in her dreamy voice, just as she had done long ago in the summerhouse.

I spent one August bank-holiday weekend on the island, having sailed down single-handed in my own boat, *Jenny Wren*. I had arranged to be back in Whiterock by Monday, but when Monday came there were heavy thunderous squalls around, sandwiched between quite pleasant sunny spells. I tried to persuade Arthur to come with me in *Margaret* or lend me Freddie's weight as ballast, but Arthur declared he needed Freddie to go with them to Killyleagh to fetch coal, that Mary wanted to shop there, and that I had much better give up the idea of Whiterock and come with them. An hour of good sailing weather slipped by as the argument went on, until it ended as it usually does between two pig-headed people, by both of us going our own way. At the last moment Mary came down the jetty, imploring me to take care and making me promise to sail under jib only. To please her I did.

I got about as far as the trees on Castle Island when I found I was completely becalmed. Under these circumstances Mary could not expect me to keep my promise and, anyhow, *Margaret* was almost out of sight at the south end of the Sound. So I put up the mainsail and with its help drew out from under the trees. From then on things began to happen. The breeze freshened in a series of squalls, each one stronger than the one before, until after a really vicious one *Jenny Wren* quietly laid her mainsail on the water. I stared incredulously as little green whirligigs of water spread over the white sail, and then as it became more dimly green, as she slowly turned completely over, I clambered on to her bottom and stood up to attract attention from the shore.

But the shore was obliterated by a solid wall of rain with dark water jabbling beneath it. Soon it was hissing all round me, leaving me almost as wet as if I had been in the sea, but as it thinned I saw the familiar red hull of *Owen Roe* coming towards me.

I was not very pleased about this episode, in fact I felt a little foolish, particularly about having broken my promise to Mary, and therefore was not overjoyed when I heard Arthur's voice on the phone a few days later.

'Just rang up to know if you got to Whiterock all right,' he said.

'No,' I said shortly.

'Capsize?' I could hear him grinning

'Yes. Did you get to Killyleagh?' I said, more wanting to change the subject than wanting to know.

'No.'

'Good heavens! You didn't capsize, did you?... Well, come on, let's hear your story.'

Their story was much better than mine, especially as told by Mary.

As the thunder squall built up behind them, Freddie kept pointing it out to Arthur and suggesting that they either reefed or took the mainsail down. But Arthur was deaf to all such suggestions. He said a lot of things that he must afterwards have regretted, such as, when Freddie said he knew of a boat just like *Margaret* which had been capsized, that it could not have been properly sailed.

When the full fury of the squall hit them, Mary said she had the strange sensation that some giant had placed his fingertip on *Margaret's* mast and was pushing her down as well as forward, so that she built up an enormous bow wave, which grew even higher than the boat itself, until quite gently it began to spill in over the gunwale. *Margaret* slewed round on her beam ends and, like *Jenny*, laid her large sail flat on the sea.

At this moment Arthur apparently felt some heroic gesture to save his family and friend was called for, so he dived overboard, intending, I suppose, to bring the dinghy to them. But as he broke surface he realized that, as the dinghy was tied to *Margaret*, he need not have bothered and, as he had his glasses on, he now could see nothing. However, they all fished him up and, pulling up the dinghy by its painter, they clambered in. But Arthur had tied the painter with one of his bird's nests, which could not be undone. Urgency was lent to their efforts, because it was not known how long *Margaret* would lie placidly on her side and when she might decide to sink. Neither Freddie nor Arthur had a knife, and Mary said that, although she offered them the only sharp thing she had — a hairpin — they did not seem to appreciate it just then.

Then she saw her shopping basket with all their ration books in it floating away.

Eventually they undid the knot and then attempted without much success to tow *Margaret* towards the shore, but fortunately their plight had also been seen and a kindly motor boat came out and took them all in tow. Only Mary's basket went to a watery grave, and afterwards, when they went to the Food Office to get new ration books, Mary said they were ushered down the corridor from one official to another for no other reason than that each official simply wanted to hear the tale of their loss at first hand.

Arthur sailing 'Margaret'

Although life on the island was pleasant on fine summer days it was never convenient. Water had to be drawn from a well and supplies to be fetched by boat from quite some distance, and with our quickly changing weather it was sometimes difficult enough to reach the island and often even more difficult to get off it again.

After a summer of this sort of picnicking existence Mary and Arthur took a house in Whiterock, and because of the petrol shortage Arthur bought a motorbicycle. They had a faithful servant Lily, a gentle, docile creature, who was despatched with Arthur each weekend and who shyly confessed to Mary that she had not felt it right to put her arms round Mr. McCabe, but after the first bump she found she had to.

There was always the utmost commotion every time they set out. First Lily, leaning forward to try to balance the enormous rucksack on her back, would be placed on the pillion, a carrier-bag of provisions laid on her lap, then Arthur would get on and balance an even larger sail-bag in front of him on the petrol tank. The machine seemed to do a great deal of back-firing before it took off, and at the last moment Shandy always managed to escape and pursue them, barking furiously as far as the railway bridge on King's Road. Once Arthur attempted to shake off Shandy by suddenly swerving into Barnett's Road, so that the poor dog, unable to turn so quickly, skidded into the bridge. The unfortunate Lily was also taken by surprise and nearly unshipped, after which she begged to be allowed to go by bus as Mary so wisely did.

Bruce was now stationed in Aberdeen, and it soon occurred to the McCabes that it would be even more convenient to live in Whiterock, and so they leased the house in Knock to the Women's Auxiliary Air Force. When asked why to the W.A.A.F.s, Arthur said because he was hoping Tommy would make one of his unannounced visits which unfortunately he never did.

Mary began the task of clearing the house for the W.A.A.F.s. It took weeks and weeks. Just what she did with all the stuff is not clear, and much of what might have been treasured by others may have gone to the bin. I have already mentioned 'the Confessional', the awkward structure at the back of the hall, and the dark narrow stairs, and Mary's struggles to negotiate these obstacles reminded me of how, long ago, Bruce had started to build a dinghy in the attic. How it was ever got down I never heard and can only conclude that it was never finished, but in manoeuvering planks round these difficulties Alan was hit in the eye. Mrs. Carey was chatting to Miss Archer in the morning-room when her youngest appeared, his eye streaming blood. She at once jumped up, asking her visitor to help her, only to find that Miss Archer was stretched on the floor in a dead faint.

The stairs proved equally difficult for Mary and in the end she tired of staggering down with armfuls from the attics and took to throwing books out of the sky-light. Many reached the ground and were picked up, but others stuck in the gutter, and many a late-night short-cutter was startled by a flutter of leaves and a soft plop as the wind brought down yet another book.

One day I dropped in to see if I could help. I discovered Mary with an enormous document spread on the floor of the hall. It was the Carey family tree which traced their ancestors right back to a Carey (then spelled 'Cary') who had married Mary Boleyn, a sister of Anne. Their grandson, Sir Robert Carey, had ridden in record time to Edinburgh with the news of Queen Elizabeth's death. Recently I learned from Christopher Hibbert's *Charles I* that this Carey was made controller of the young Prince Charles' household. At the time of James I's accession the Prince was only three years old, a weakly child who could neither walk nor talk properly, and he was given into the care of Sir Robert's wife with suggestions that his legs should be put into splints and a ligament of his tongue cut. Fortunately Lady Carey paid no heed to these gruesome instructions, and under her care, which extended until he was twelve, the future Charles I grew into a normal, though not a very robust, young boy. It was only after the death of his elder brother that he became the heir presumptive, and the guardian of his early years was rewarded by being buried in Westminster Abbey.

The first governor of the Falkland Islands was a Carey and was created Viscount Falkland but that branch of the family died out with the second viscount. Had I read Joyce Cary's books at that time I could have seen if he were connected. These were things which the Careys never bothered to tell you about themselves, but it possibly explains why they remained impervious to the cuts and slights that other people inflict on each other as they struggle up the social ladder, and why the thought of entering the competitive rat-race of the material world never appealed to them.

When the day of the move finally came, the removal men also had their troubles with the stairs. They went to Mary and said they had tried every method known to furniture removers to get a large wardrobe past an ornamental knob at the foot of the bannisters and they wondered how the wardrobe had ever been got up the stairs.

'Oh yes,' said Mary, 'I remember that was put there later. Well, we'll soon fix that,' and returning with a saw, she did.

It was not unusual to find Mary's wake strewn with people rendered utterly speechless.

21

Here, if I may, I would like to digress a little.

I had become secretary to the German Refugee Committee in Belfast, and one of my duties was to make the holiday arrangements for the children under its care. Most of the children managed this perfectly well for themselves by being invited to the homes of their school fellows, but from time to time there was someone who had nowhere to go between two invitations. There was also the complication of those who became eighteen. So long as you were under eighteen, you were a harmless refugee child and allowed to go to the seaside, but the minute you were eighteen you were an enemy alien and not allowed within twenty miles of the sea without a special permit. The police and the Home Office were always very reasonable about granting permits, but it took time and a lot of writing. And often when the whole thing seemed fixed, somebody in the hostess's family took measles, the dates were altered, and the whole process had to be begun again. Many a time I looked ruefully at those advertisements appealing to the nation to save paper, and wondered if all these regulations ever really hampered a Nazi agent or only those prepared to observe them.

By the summer of 1942 the idea of having a camp somewhere on the west side of Strangford Lough, which was outside the Prohibited Area, seemed to me to be not only a paper saving, but from the secretary's point of view, a labour saving device as well. Somewhere with barns and outbuildings, because we had no tents.

Miss Baillie who lived in Ringdufferin House had recently died and the place would soon be sold. I had often seen it from the sea and knew it had wonderful outbuildings, so I got in touch with the solicitors, and with the necessary permission in my pocket set off one afternoon to look over the yard and make final arrangements.

It was one of those days when big clouds move slowly and the Mournes looked very blue and clear, leaving the Lough breathlessly still and silver. I walked down from the bus, and as I turned in through the gates, I fell under the enchantment of that place, as I have done every time I have gone there since. The drive, grass-grown in the middle, followed the edge of the Lough in a gentle curve with beautiful specimen trees on either side, and you could almost hear the whirl of Victorian equipages sweeping gracefully along it. The house, when it came in sight, was disappointing, being rather squat, two-storied in front and dropping to three at the back.

Mary, the old housekeeper, opened the door and was delighted to see me as I think she would have been delighted to see anyone. Not many people had come down that drive since Miss Baillie passed up it. She insisted in showing me all over the house with all the pride of an old servant in her mistress's possessions.

'And this is the room we call the India Room,' she said, showing me into an ice-cold, north-facing bedroom, 'this is where they kept all the dolls and things the old master sent them from India.' And there it was, the most fantastic collection of Victorian playthings. Miss Baillie and her two sisters had lived to a good age, they had never married and, it seemed, had rarely moved outside the gates, apart from their annual holiday when they went to stay in Jury's hotel in Dublin because they 'so enjoyed the noise'. Here in this room were preserved intact all the amusements and pastimes of their youth. I am happy to say that the present owners of the house have also preserved these things, but now in a special room in the basement.

'Many's the time Miss Louie wrought in them flower beds,' said Mary. I was enjoying Mary and her use of English and would have loved to let her go on but had to keep reminding her that it was really the stableyard I had come to look at. Eventually she released me to William James, but insisted that I should come to the kitchen for a cup of tea before starting back for the bus.

As Mary poured the tea, I said what a lovely old place it was and how I had often looked at it from the sea when sailing past.

'Oh dear,' said Mary, 'that's very dangerous. Does your mother know you go sailing? Why, only last summer...' and here she unfolded the tale of *Margaret's* mishap, which also lost nothing in the telling by this Mary, ending with 'and that very same day there was another young lady that had been with them on the island, and she set out to sail her lone, the poor foolish creature, and the same great storm came down and upset her too. And there she was clinging on with not a one to see her or to hear her but the screeching gulls.'

I could hardly drink my tea for concern at this young woman's plight. I just hadn't the heart to tell her it had not been a bit like that really.

22

When all the arrangements for the camp had been completed, I asked Arthur if they would be on the island that weekend and if the advance party, that was myself and a fourteen year old girl called Inge, could stay there too.

'Sure,' said Arthur, 'give a shout from Ringhaddy pier and somebody will come over for you.'

I had borrowed from kind friends, who in peace time would have been cruising in Scotland at this time of year, some twenty sleeping bags. Inge and I loaded these and an assortment of large pots and pans into my car and we set off for Ringdufferin. We left the car in the yard and, taking some belongings and provisions in a rucksack, we walked round to Ringhaddy pier. It was further than I thought and nearly nine o'clock when we got there. The house across the water looked deserted, its windows blankly reflecting the setting sun. We shouted and hallooed, but nothing stirred on the island, so we went a little farther and borrowed a boat from the Farrell's farm, a heavy, cumbersome boat with oars that felt like telegraph poles. I doubt if Inge had ever been in a boat before, or at least one like this, but she cheerfully accepted this rather roundabout way of getting to the island. She was a gentle, governess-reared daughter of a Hamburg doctor.

'But how shall we get in without a key?' she asked with a certain practicality. I had been wondering about that too, but hoped that with any luck we might find the house unlocked. This time, however, the doors were locked and bolted. I started poking at a loose window catch, whilst Inge kept up an admiring commentary. I was obviously the first house breaker she had ever seen in action, and I felt I could not let her down.

We got in eventually and slept well, but next morning the wind had freshened and I thought we should get off the island before it got worse, without waiting to see if Arthur would arrive.

We drove round to Whiterock, and as we turned in at the gate, I said to Inge: 'These friends of mine are a little unusual, so don't be surprised at anything that may happen.'

Shandy barked as Mary came to the door with a half-eaten bun in her hand. She immediately crammed the rest of the bun into her mouth, made some incoherent squawks and, rushing upstairs, began to wave a red evening dress out of the window, at the same time banging on the sill with a saucepan lid. Inge looked at me a little uncertainly.

When Mary at length came down and Shandy had been persuaded to stop barking, she explained that all had been peace and serenity until, on bringing Arthur his breakfast tray, she had remarked on the loveliness of the morning and wondered if I would be coming down for a sail. At which Arthur said 'Oh my God' and jumped out of bed.

'I never liked language like that,' said Mary, 'but that he should say that at the thought of your coming to see us quite shocked me.'

He had completely forgotten the arrangement, and as he pulled on his clothes and gobbled his breakfast, he instructed Mary that, if by any chance I should turn up at the house before he had set sail, she was to give him a signal. And so she did.

The camp was a great success, although for Inge after this beginning it may have seemed a little tame. Arthur sailed over to see us the following weekend and took relays of campers out in *Margaret*.

I was disappointed to find, when we held our first sing-song, that the children who had now been in this country for three or four years had forgotten their German songs, in fact the only song the boys seemed to know was 'Deep in the heart of Texas', which they sang so as to drown everybody else. I appealed to some of the older campers to re-teach them their own songs. The children — I call them that collectively, although their ages ranged from eighteen or nineteen down to eight — 'the campers' responded readily and soon Texas had slipped in the charts and we had built up a repertoire of songs which could have been heard in any German youth hostel before the war.

People in the neighbourhood were very kind to us, asking us out to tea, and as a small return we gave our little recital before we left. Mr. Utitz, himself a refugee, showed us over the leather factory in Shrigley and his mother gave us tea in their small house in Killyleagh.

At that time the American army was stationed in Killyleagh, and as we trooped out of the house, a sergeant came over and became interested in the children.

'But where are all their parents?' he asked.

'Somewhere in Germany or Austria,' I said.

'Aw the pore lil' kids.' He disappeared into his billet and came back, his helmet brimming with slabs of chocolate and sweets.

So there in the middle of the street, like a little group of out-of-season carol-singers, we sang our songs, surrounded by the soldiers, and some bemused natives of Killyleagh.

I have mentioned this incident because, although it does not really concern the Careys, it is one of my pleasanter memories of the war. Another is of the last night of our camp, when Mary had invited us all to picnic on the island. It was a lovely, wind-still evening and as we rowed back in the dark, still singing, the phosphorescence rippled in the wake and dripped like jewels from the blades of the oars.

23

Soon after this Arthur decided that a boat with a cabin would be an advantage, so he sold *Margaret* and bought a boat called *Lurline*. There were two disadvantages about *Lurline*. One was that she had been laid up 'for the duration' and was therefore at the farthermost corner of the boatyard; the other, that she had a most enormous, almost triangular, keel like a child's toy boat, so that, added to the normal hazards that a boat may fall over sideways when being moved, there was also the possibility that *Lurline* could nose-dive or tip up backwards. From which it may be gathered that I never really cared for *Lurline*.

However, we all rallied round to help Arthur launch this monster and as we laboured, and that is the right word for it, since it seemed to involve moving every boat in the yard, Mary would stumble towards us, bearing pots of tea.

At last the time of the launch was fixed for two o'clock one Saturday afternoon, but then there were hitches and delays, so that we missed the tide. The next favourable time would be between two and three on Sunday morning, so we spent a pleasant evening of Carey games in the house at Whiterock, before re-assembling on the slipway in the dark.

Ronald and Philip were in charge of the operation and they put Arthur on to the winch with instructions to be sure to take the handles off and only to apply the brake if Ronald said so, but because it is sometimes difficult for the person on the winch to hear what is happening outside, I was posted at the entrance of the shed to pass on alarms if genuine. Launching a boat is always a nerve-racking business, even in daylight, but at two in the morning under black-out conditions, whereby even torches had to be screened by tissue paper, it is just that much worse.

Slowly the dark bulk of *Lurline* began to shudder and creak, and the wire warp slithered out past my feet. I had sometimes wondered what would happen if that wire ever broke. It was led through between the props supporting all the boats in the shed, and if it recoiled, I imagined the whole place would fold together like a pack of cards. However, I tried to keep such forebodings from my mind as *Lurline* began her journey to the sea.

As she gathered momentum, the rumbling and grinding of iron wheels on iron rails and the squealing and clanking of the winch increased in a steady crescendo, until suddenly from inside the shed came a terrible bang. Without waiting to see what might happen next, I moved myself about twenty yards along the shore. When I turned round, *Lurline* was trundling to a halt at the foot of the slipway, and everyone was cautiously approaching the shed.

'You all right, Arthur?' we asked.

'Yes,' came a rather doubtful voice from the darkness.

'What on earth was that bang?'

'Can't think.'

We searched by the light of our dimmed torches, but found nothing amiss.

Next morning, when the incoming tide had successfully lifted *Lurline* off her carriage, we were about to pack up, when the old Colonel appeared, making one of his Sunday morning tours of inspection.

'Here, look at this,' he said.

A curious beehive-like hump had appeared on the corrugated iron roof of the shed.

'Been done from the inside,' he said in a moment of perspicacity.

We went inside. The dent was just above the winch.

'Arthur,' we said, 'did you take off both handles last night?'

'Are there two?' he said.

Certainly some guardian angel worked overtime on Arthur.

24

Mary and Arthur enjoyed living in Whiterock although the house was very different to Brugh. It had been designed by Philip, a mutual friend, who was not only an architect but a designer of boats as well, and much care and thought had been given to the planning of its interior. 'I suppose I ought really to be more appreciative,' said Mary, 'but I find Philip has made a place for everything.'

During those war years a bus removed most of the male population at eight in the morning and brought them back at seven at night, and as this was the only bus that passed that way, it left the women folk to themselves all day. Once a military motorcyclist's machine broke down just outside Mary's gate and she and others went down to him, Mary bearing her usual cup of tea. He expressed his thanks and surprise at their kindness and interest in him, to which Mary said: 'But you've no idea what an event you are for us.'

Mary was always interested in people, in all sorts of people, and frequently got involved in conversations in improbable places. She was genuinely kind, yet for all her gentle manner she was shrewd and not deceived by self-opinionated people. She had a wide, serene forehead with curiously hooded eyelids, and when she smiled her eyes almost closed, but sometimes from beneath those eyelids you caught the glint of mischief. She could gauge to a nicety the degree of humour anyone possessed and the length to which she might pull a leg, yet it was all done so subtly and her remarks appeared so guileless that I doubt if her victims ever realized what was afoot.

After the war was over the W.A.A.F.s gave up their lease of the

The Careys

house. Bruce, who had married in Aberdeen, decided to settle there, so he was no longer interested in the house and Mary and Arthur then decided to sell it. This was a great grief to me as I had always thought that some day they would come back again, and at first I could hardly grasp that other people with other furniture and other pictures would be living permanently in the house I knew so well.

By this time Arthur had realized that *Lurline's* deep keel was even more of an obstruction to his navigation than *Margaret's* retractable centre-plate had been, so he sold her and bought a boat of reasonable dimensions, called *Alskling*, which also had a centre-plate. At once he was full of enthusiasm, as he always was for any new project, making plans for where they would sail and what they would do with her. *Alskling* was not a large boat. She had two cabins, a main one which could sleep two, and a small one in the bow.

They began by making one or two short trips down the Irish coast and across to the Isle of Man. Then, with Glen to help as crew they set out on their first cruise round the south of Ireland.

I doubt if Mary ever really enjoyed cruising. She had enjoyed sailing around Strangford on sunny afternoons, but cruising is another matter. To those who enjoy cruising it presents a challenge, rather as Everest does; it has its hazards and its hardships, but with careful planning and a realization of what is likely to befall much misery can be avoided. It is also very important to know when the time has come to be frightened and when what seems alarming is the fairly normal behaviour of boats. Some people have a natural instinct for this, others acquire it by experience, and Mary may be excused for never having been able to make the distinction because she only began sailing in her late forties.

She wrote an account of their voyage but strangely enough Mary, who could describe things so vividly and amusingly when talking to you, became sadly restrained when writing them down. Gone is her verbal description of Arthur's attempt to seal a leak in the centre-board casing with tallow, until overcome with the smell of the tallow, the bilge and the motion of the boat he 'lay stretched on his bunk like a Crusader on a tomb'. Or how he had been reading a paper-back thriller and had left it on top of his precious charts, which were very hard to get so soon after the war, and how an enormous wave had lifted the hatch and poured down over the table. When Arthur saw how the dye from the book had stained his charts he was so disgusted that he threw the book overboard, and so, as Mary said, 'for the rest of the trip he never knew whodunnit.'

Instead her chronicle has many references to being cold, wet, sea-sick and frightened and I can only marvel at how she managed to endure it all. For endure she did, like a faithful spaniel which does not appreciate music yet feels compelled to sit under the piano close to its master's feet. She described how they would listen to the weather report, and how she knew it must be serious because Glen took his teeth out and put them carefully away. 'The insurance people are a bit sticky about paying for teeth lost overboard through sea-sickness.'

Yet not all the entries in her chronicle recorded privation. Sometimes the sun shone and the sea smiled. Glen seems to have left them, possibly at Dun Laoghaire, for they seemed to have sailed to Cork by themselves with Mary faithfully steering for a steamer under the impression that it was the lightship Arthur had told her to aim for. She was very short-sighted. In Cork they picked up Emily, who was about twelve then, and they went to Kerry, but there it rained incessantly and the chronicle ends abruptly when Mary decided to take Emily home by train. It is not explained how Arthur brought the boat up north again. Maybe he sailed back single-handed as far as Arklow, because next year, in 1948, when he sailed right round Ireland with Tom as crew, they started from Arklow.

Mary did not go with them and ironically they enjoyed very good weather and had a smooth passage almost devoid of incident. In Valentia an elderly English lady whom they met in the bar of the hotel begged to be taken with them up the west coast, an idea which struck Tom speechless with horror so that he disappeared at once. Arthur managed to extricate himself with stealth and, meeting up with Tom, they decided to leave immediately, but just as they were casting off, their acquaintance appeared on the quay-side and burst into tears at being so basely deserted. After that deplorable incident they spent the next two nights at sea in the safety and solitude of the Atlantic.

Only once were they storm-bound in Belmullet, which Arthur described as a dirty, depressing town, but which redeemed itself when they discovered some bottles of claret in a shop. The proprietor was delighted to let them have the lot cheap, saying there was no demand for claret in Belmullet.

From then on it was plain sailing and they made the trip from Arklow to Cultra in three weeks, unaccompanied by any of the hair-raising episodes which used to attend Arthur's voyages. He had come a long way since those early beginnings.

Possibly it was the success of this trip that encouraged Mary to try again when Arthur and Tom planned a cruise to France the following year. Arthur said her French would be very useful when they got there and that as he and Tom had now proved their proficiency there was no need to be so frightened. Mary said that it was just as well that Tom had served in submarines in the war because there was not much room in *Alskling's* forward cabin.

Anyhow they set sail once again and reached the Scilly Isles without incident, although really by accident. Arthur had intended to go to Falmouth, but rounding the Lizard had encountered such a ferocious tide racing down the English Channel that, rather than battle against it, he decided to turn round and go with it to the Scillies instead. Mary was delighted and not a little surprised when they turned up almost where they ought to be, as she had begun to think that if they missed them, it might be a long time before they saw land again.

The people she found very kind and friendly. 'The Scillonians,' she corrected me afterwards, 'they don't like being called Scilly Islanders.' Then the Customs man came down and after inspecting them asked if there was anything he could do for them. They said they would love a bath, and he led them to his house. After that, Mary said the attitude of the people was noticeably cooler; if you are a friend of the Customs man you are no friend of a Scillonian.

They reached Brittany safely and Mary set off to buy provisions. Fearing that her French might be a little rusty she thought she would first ask if they spoke English, but by a slip of the tongue she said 'Parlez-vous Francais?' — 'But yes,' said the shopkeeper in a rather strange version of the language, 'although I am a Breton, I can speak French,' and Mary realized with a sinking heart that French might not be a mother tongue for either of them. However, she managed to make her purchases without too much sign language, and they ate delicious meals both on board and in little quay-side restaurants. Mary had such an intense interest in people that I think had she landed in Outer Mongolia she would have carried on a conversation somehow. Even, as Arthur said, if she went ashore on the simplest errand it always seemed to embroil the whole village, who frequently came back to the boat with her.

Mary enjoyed every moment of her return visit to France, but the weather was so hot that at night *Alskling* was like an oven, so that in the end they were quite glad to put to sea again, even although poor Mary never succeeded in growing sea-legs.

25

I was another of those daughters of Knockdene Park, already mentioned, who had brought their husbands to live in the same houses in which they themselves had been born, and in due course my first-born arrived, but as Mary did not often come up from Whiterock she did not come to see the baby until the baby was old enough to see her. We went into the rose garden to the pram and as Mary bent smilingly over it, the baby stopped sucking her thumb and studied Mary blandly and unblinkingly. At which Mary withdrew saying: 'Ah yes dear, *you* have poise.'

We wandered back into the house through the kitchen and Mary looked up at the two sets of pulley lines which hung from the ceiling. Ours was an old-fashioned, high-ceilinged kitchen which could hang aloft an entire week's washing without inconveniencing anyone below. 'I see you've kept your pulley lines,' said Mary. 'I had ours taken down because people just would hang things on them.' I suppose she meant Arthur and his wet sails.

Mary made most of her trips to Belfast by bus and got friendly, as was her way with everyone, with the conductors. Once she appeared with one of them on his day off saying: 'This is Tommy. I've brought him along to see your lovely garden.' But Mary was remembering our garden as it was in my parents' day, when we had a regular and skilled gardener, something the garden had not seen for many a long year. Tommy looked around him and said: 'Aye, the weeds is dasprit,' which was honest anyway.

We always went to see Mary and Arthur when we went to Whiterock, although as our family increased to three little girls and we sold the boat, our visits became less frequent. Then one day in the autumn of 1950 Mary said that Arthur was in bed with jaundice, but that we should go up and see him. We found him very lively, full of enthusiasm for a new piece of equipment Radio Development were now stocking, a tape recorder. We all had to say something to it and then he would play it back, and we were appalled at what we sounded like. Every time he bounced out of bed to adjust the machine, Mary raised deploring eyes to heaven. He was supposed to be resting before going into hospital for examination.

I thought Arthur looked a strange colour, but I never thought that that would be the last time I would see him. He died in hospital a few months later.

It was then that I was really sorry that the house in Knock had been sold. It would have been so much easier to drop in to see Mary to cheer her up, although when I did so at Whiterock I often came away cheerier than I went. She had a way of looking at life that I always enjoyed, of turning the most common-place happenings into something entertaining and amusing. Emily by now was becoming a grown-up young lady and wanting to stretch her wings, and there must have been times when Mary was lonely, yet I never found her being sorry for herself.

Since I have begun to put this book together I have been talking to many people who knew the Careys, and of Mary they all say the same thing. How kind she was to everyone no matter who they were and the interest she took in them as individuals, the tramp in the summerhouse, the van-driver who crashed through the gate, the soldier whose machine broke down or the bus conductor on his day off, they all were given a cup of tea and friendly chat which Mary genuinely enjoyed too.

As you grow older you realise sadly that things which you have always taken for granted will one day change and that no magic can put the clock back. I think I first became aware of this when Brugh was sold and I realized that I should never again see Mary and Arthur against that familiar background, and again after Arthur's death, when *Alskling* was sold, that there would never again be any more daft escapades in boats, yet somehow I never imagined that one day Mary might be only a memory. I was occupied with our young family and did not see her as often as I might have wished, but I knew she was there and that I had only to go to Whiterock to enjoy her company once more. Then, quite suddenly, six years after Arthur she died.

Knockdene Park looks just the same as it did when I was a child. The houses are the same and the trees and all that seclusion of privet hedge. My children have ridden their tricycles down its uneven, unflagged paths over the same bumps. It is true that the gas lamps have gone, that the milk now comes clinking in a lorry, the bread growls round in an electric van, and I doubt if any butcher delivers anything at all, much less in a smart equipage with a high-stepping pony. Yet these are only minor changes.

The one great difference is that the Careys no longer live there, nor, except for Alan in America, do they live anywhere else, save only in the memories of those fortunate enough to have known them.